Dear Brooks,

Always remember these fantastic and exciting days of exquisite intellect and work.

Always,
Luella Brayton
March 23-25, 1997

Brooks,

Thanks for efficient & pleasant transport - Good luck.

James Tobin

Brooks,

Thanks for all the hospitality and best wishes for the future

Thanks for everything

The World Economy in Transition

Best
Mandl

Franco Modigliani
3/25/20

The World Economy in Transition

What Leading Economists Think

Edited by

Randall Hinshaw

Edward Elgar
Cheltenham, UK • Brookfield, US

Published by
Edward Elgar Publishing Limited
8 Lansdown Place
Cheltenham
Glos GL50 2HU
UK

Edward Elgar Publishing Company
Old Post Road
Brookfield
Vermont 05036
US

British Library Cataloguing in Publication Data

World Economy in Transition: What Leading Economists Think
  I. Hinshaw, Randall
  330.9

Library of Congress Cataloguing in Publication Data

The world economy in transition : what leading economists think /
  edited by Randall Hinshaw.
    Includes indexes.
    1. Economic history—1990–.   2. Economic policy.   I. Hinshaw,
  Randall Weston.
  HC59.15.W664   1996
  330.9—dc20   95–30782
                                                                    CIP

ISBN 1 85898 343 6

Typeset by Manton Typesetters, 5–7 Eastfield Road, Louth, Lincs LN11 7AJ, UK
Printed and bound in Great Britain by
Biddles Limited, Guildford and King's Lynn

Contents

Contributors

SVEN W. ARNDT, Professor of Economics and Director, The Lowe Institute of Political Economy, Claremont McKenna College

ANSLEY J. COALE, Professor of Economics Emeritus, Princeton University; former Director, Princeton Office of Population Research

RICHARD N. COOPER (Chairman), Maurits C. Boas Professor of International Economics, Harvard University; former Under Secretary of State for Economic Affairs

W.M. CORDEN, Professor of International Economics, The Paul H. Nitze School of Advanced International Studies, The Johns Hopkins University

ROBERT H. EVANS, Director, The Johns Hopkins University Bologna Center

JEFFREY A. FRANKEL, Professor of Economics, University of California, Berkeley

RANDALL HINSHAW, Professor of Economics Emeritus, The Claremont Graduate School

CHRISTOPHER JOHNSON, United Kingdom Adviser, Association for the Monetary Union of Europe

PAUL W. McCRACKEN, Edmund Ezra Day Distinguished Professor Emeritus, The University of Michigan; former Chairman, President's Council of Economic Advisers

LIONEL W. McKENZIE, Wilson Professor of Economics Emeritus, University of Rochester

BAILEY MORRIS, Editor, *Economic Insights*, Institute for International Economics

ROBERT A. MUNDELL, Professor of Economics, Columbia University

Foreword

In late January 1994, when the United States was beginning to recover from many months of economic recession, The Claremont Graduate School, in cooperation with the other Claremont Colleges, staged the twelfth in the 'Bologna–Claremont' series of dialogues on domestic and international monetary issues. The sixteen participants included three Nobel Laureates in Economics, other leading economists, and former top government officials. The series, in which five meetings have been in Europe, originated in 1967 at the Johns Hopkins University Bologna Center. Robert Evans, the present director of the Center, honored the 1994 conference by coming to Claremont as a ceremonial representative.

Because of the end of the Cold War and the resulting extensive cuts in US defense expenditures, the recession, with its accompanying unemployment, was particularly severe in southern California, where the meeting took place. Unemployment, however, was a serious problem not only in the United States but also in Western Europe, where high levels of unemployment had become chronic. This widespread problem was one of the main topics discussed during the two-day meeting, and was the subject of the meeting's only prepared paper: the third Robbins Memorial Lecture delivered by Nobel Laureate Robert M. Solow on the topic, 'Is All That European Unemployment Necessary?'. Forty-eight hours after its delivery, the lecture was cited by conference member Bailey Morris in her column in the London *Independent*, and the next day a request for copies came from Number 10 Downing Street. The lecture, which is reproduced at the end of this volume, was dedicated to the eminent British economist and public figure, Lord Robbins, who moderated seven of the conferences and whose son, the Honourable Richard Robbins, attended

the Claremont meeting. A second guest of honor was Clarice
Thorp, the widow of Ambassador Willard Long Thorp, the founding chairman of the series.

A conference of this scope requires many weeks of prepara-
tion and the assistance of people far too numerous to identify. It
would be unpardonable, however, not to acknowledge the contributions of a few key persons. The Claremont Graduate School's
Professor of Economics Emeritus, Randall Hinshaw, present at
the creation of the series and its true parent, once again dreamed,
dared, designed and sustained this remarkable event. Of Randall
Hinshaw: *sine qua non*. Deep appreciation is owed indeed to the
dialogue participants, most of whom came to Claremont from
long distances – two from abroad. For the fourth time, Harvard
Professor Richard Cooper chaired the meeting with his usual rare
skill. With characteristic wisdom, attention to detail, and grace
under pressure, Luzma Brayton, the Graduate School's Director
of Special Events, spent countless hours in conference planning.

As at the preceding five conferences held in Claremont, the
1994 meeting took place on the beautiful campus of Scripps
College, whose staff, under the leadership of President Nancy
Bekavac, was exceptionally cooperative and efficient in assuring
the smooth running of the physical arrangements. Through the
good offices of Jeanette Magee of its Department of Economics,
Pomona College made available without charge the handsome
auditorium in which Professor Solow's public lecture was delivered. And as at the 1991 Claremont conference, Alex Huemer, a
doctoral candidate, organized a highly efficient student taxi service for the participants.

In the days immediately following the conference, a stream of
letters arrived in Claremont attesting to the meeting's success. In
his letter, Yale Nobel Laureate James Tobin wrote, 'I greatly
enjoyed your conference and learned from it. The free-form framework, under Cooper's expert yet gentle moderatorship, worked
very well. I hope Paul Samuelson's stories will be preserved for
posterity'.

Let me assure Professor Tobin that Paul Samuelson's stories
have been immortalized in this volume, as well as the marvelous

conversations of a most remarkable group of economists. They quicken my desire for another such gathering as soon as possible!

John David Maguire
President
The Claremont Graduate School

1. Introduction

Randall Hinshaw

This book is a lightly edited tape recording of the twelfth dialogue in what has become widely known as the Bologna–Claremont series of dialogues on current economic issues. The two-day meeting took place in Claremont, California, in late January 1994, twenty-seven years after the first meeting held at the Johns Hopkins University Bologna Center in January 1967. The 1994 group was of exceptional distinction, and included three Nobel Laureates in Economics: Professors Paul A. Samuelson and Robert M. Solow of MIT and Yale Professor James Tobin.

A few words about the conference format. The meetings have been properly described as 'conversations' among leading economists. With the exception of the opening public lecture, about which more below, there are no prepared papers. Instead, under the guidance of Professor Richard N. Cooper, who with rare skill has chaired the last four dialogues, an agenda is worked out at the opening session involving a few subtopics suggested by the conference theme. A member particularly qualified on a given subtopic is asked by the chairman to introduce the discussion on that subject, which later becomes a chapter in the book. Members are seated around a U-shaped table, and all statements are made sitting down.

Editing has been limited to removing grammatical slips and, in a very few cases, points that were not clear to the editor. To ensure the integrity of the dialogue, no effort was made to rearrange the statements, all of which are in the order in which they were made. As always at these meetings, the 1994 discussion was good-humored and frequently accompanied by smiles and laughter. In a few but not all cases, the often loud laughter has been indicated in brackets.

The relaxed and flexible format is undoubtedly largely responsible for the longevity of the series. The one drawback, or possibly virtue, is that, regardless of the announced theme, each dialogue takes on a life of its own. On the printed program, the stated theme of the 1994 meeting was 'Domestic and International Macroeconomic Issues in Key Countries'. At the opening session, however, it became clear that the group did not want the discussion to be limited to 'key' countries, however that somewhat ambiguous word is defined, but decided to include the world as a whole, though certain areas – notably North America, Western Europe and Japan – received considerably more attention than others.

No attempt will here be made to summarize the dialogue, which eloquently speaks for itself, but a comment or two may be in order. A principal subtopic was the widespread problem of chronic unemployment, which has been particularly acute in Europe. European unemployment was the subject of the third Robbins Memorial Lecture honoring the memory of the late Lord Robbins, the eminent British economist and statesman who served as moderator of seven of the dialogues. The lecture, delivered by Professor Solow on the eve of the conference, was open to the public, and is reproduced as the final chapter of this volume under the title 'Is All That European Unemployment Necessary?'.

The 1994 dialogue took place at a time when the United States was recovering from many months of recession. Unemployment, which had peaked at 7.7 percent in June 1992, had dropped to 6.7 percent in January 1994, the month of the conference. In California, however, where the meeting took place, the unemployment rate, mainly because of massive defense cutbacks, was much higher; it was 10.1 percent at the time of the conference and has since dropped only slightly.

This situation raised an important question of policy, particularly for the Federal Reserve. Under the Clinton program of deficit reduction, fiscal stimulus was ruled out as a means of promoting recovery. The alternative form of stimulus was monetary policy. At the time of the meeting, short-term interest rates were at low levels, and Professor Tobin expressed the view that the Fed could best promote recovery by refraining from raising those rates. Somewhat facetiously, Professor Solow remarked that since fiscal stimulus had been ruled out, the only other alternative to monetary stimulus was prayer!

Any hopes that the Federal Reserve would continue to hold short-term interest rates at the low levels prevailing at the beginning of the year were soon frustrated. In a series of steps, the Federal Reserve did raise short-term interest rates substantially during most of 1994 because of concern that the US economy might be overheating. In earlier years, an unemployment rate of 4 percent had been regarded as an 'inflation-safe' lower limit, but later studies have concluded that this figure should be revised upward to 6 percent or even higher. The Federal Reserve, always inflation conscious, may have been influenced by the fact that the national unemployment rate might be falling below the inflation-safe limit. But the upward movement of short-term interest rates and mortgage rates was a serious blow to depressed California, which accounts for about one-seventh of US gross domestic product. Unemployment in California remains much higher than in the rest of the nation and, by some measures, the state has not recovered from the 1990–91 recession.

Various other difficult and often controversial matters were discussed at the meeting – notably the issue of European monetary union, the policy questions stemming from the economic downturn in Japan, problems in the former communist countries, developments in the dubiously called Third World, and what, if anything, should at present be done about the far from ideal existing international monetary system. It would be presumptuous and completely unnecessary, however, to delay any further the conversations of the remarkably able group assembled in Claremont.

2. A Survey of Macroeconomic Trouble Spots

Introduced by Robert A. Mundell

Chairman Richard N. Cooper: My role here is as moderator or, as one might put it, traffic cop to make sure that the traffic remains at least semi-orderly. And in pursuing the compromise between order and intense interaction, I suggest that we follow what I still think of as the 'Machlup Rule' – that is to say, if you would like to speak, indicate to me by waving your name plate or moving your hand, and I will keep a list, but if there is something that was just said that provokes you to want to respond at once, put up two hands or wave wildly, and I will call on you next. But there is a condition for this ability to interrupt: you have to keep your remarks on that particular point and be brief; then I will resume my list.

Our first task this morning is to decide what we're going to talk about. The program says 'Domestic and International Macro-economic Issues in Key Countries'. There's a delightful vagueness and generality in that title. It permits a lot of scope. I suppose that as a minimum we've got to talk about domestic macroeconomic policy in the United States, in Japan and in the major European countries, including the interactions among them. But just how we do that is up to us, and Bob Mundell has agreed to lead off by making a few suggestions and observations, after which I would invite the rest of you to comment on Bob's remarks and decide how you want to proceed from there.

Robert A. Mundell: I think a topic we should certainly consider is the problem that Bob Solow talked about last night: the phenomenal increase in unemployment rates in the OECD area. This is a major problem, and we have to find a way to deal with it. As Bob laid out last night, we have one kind of Keynesian unemployment that can be corrected by expansionary policies. We have another kind of unemployment that's due to policies to pay people for not working. Welfare programs – what role have they played in the creation of very high unemployment rates? And then there's the kind of structural unemployment that we've had for a very long time in parts of Spain, in southern Italy and elsewhere. There's a lot to talk about on this topic in view of the experience of all the different countries, and it's a topic made to order for this conference.

A second topic, separate in a way, is the role of the European Community, particularly in relation to its goal of European monetary union. We have talked about this before, but it would be interesting to share ideas of why the European Monetary System broke up, what went wrong with it, what the next steps are going to be, what the future is, and also what goes on past that future in terms of the relations of the European Community as a monetary area – if it becomes that – with the rest of the world. That's a fairly self-contained topic, and we can treat it as a second issue.

A third issue is US macroeconomic policy. What about the monetary-fiscal policy mix? What about the budget deficit? What about the current-account deficit? How serious is it? Should we be worried about it? And what is the outlook for the United States over the rest of the 1990s? Are we in a period of longer-run forces that are operating on the economy that go outside the immediate purview of policy? Demographic factors – what role will they play? So US macroeconomic policy is a third category.

A fourth suggestion would be to talk about the post-Cold War world in the most general sense. I mean by that certainly the policies, dilemmas, problems and challenges thrown out by the breakup of the Soviet Union. What role should the West be playing in that and in Eastern Europe also? There are a few countries in Eastern Europe – certainly Poland, the Czech Republic and Hungary – that are lining up for getting into the European Community. And certainly the Baltic countries would like to move into the Community, but it doesn't look as if the

Community is going to let them join in anything like full-fledged status, probably not before the year 2000 and maybe much later. In the meantime, what kind of trade and monetary arrangements should the countries of Eastern Europe and the former Soviet Union have? I don't think we should spend much time on these countries, but just as part of a general discussion of the rest of the world economy.

I think we might devote the final hour to something we've always talked about at these conferences from the very beginning: reform of the international monetary system – if that's needed – and what the opportunities and prospects are.

Robert Solomon: I can't help reacting right away, saying first that I think what Bob has outlined constitutes an excellent series of topics for discussion, but there is one important gap. I don't see how we can have this conference without talking about what's called the Third World and the changes that are going on in the developing countries, including their relationship to the countries Bob is concerned with. I could elaborate, but that's enough for now.

Bailey Morris: I'd just like to follow on that. I think a good issue for us would be looking at growth trends in the world today and trying to see whether there is a shifting of these trends from the traditional industrial economies to the developing countries. I think the comments we've heard this morning will allow us to consider that question and also to look at the notion of structural decline, if there is such.

Robert H. Evans: Very briefly – again to follow up on what has just been mentioned – it seems to me that one of the great difficulties or imperatives of American foreign policy today is convincing our European allies that we are still concerned with Europe and not only with the Pacific. And it strikes me that in a discussion of the economic situation, the two may need to be dealt with somewhat hand in hand.

Cooper: Speaking of the Pacific, Japan is a very important country in the world, and we have a visitor with us from Japan. I think we want to spend some time on Japan, particularly since that country seems to be entering a period quite different from what we've come to take for granted over the last thirty years. On another matter, we have just completed the framework for what is the century's most important negotiations for the trading system, the Uruguay Round. At some point if there's time, we may want to refer to this development, which ties in with Bob Solomon's suggestion about bringing in the Third World.

Mundell: Richard, what's the Second World? I thought the Third World has ended because there is no longer a Second World.

Cooper: The old-fashioned Second World is down to Cuba and North Korea, with China suspended between the two worlds. The Second World is gradually being squeezed out.

Christopher Johnson: Can we say that Russia has joined the Third World?

Cooper: No, but I appreciate the sentiment. I've always thought the Third World was like the category 'services' in our own economy – a collective that is too big and too diverse to be very helpful.

Bob Solow cannot be with us tomorrow, so I think we should discuss things in which he has a comparative advantage today. One of those, building on his talk last night – and this was Bob Mundell's first suggestion – is the unemployment problem, which is visibly most acute in Europe. Unhappily, our anticipated visitor from Germany, Helmut Hesse, informed Randall a few days ago that he would not be able to join us because of illness. However, I was in Frankfurt last week, and talked with several members of the Bundesbank Council, so perhaps at an appropriate moment I can give my understanding – which may be imperfect and certainly is not very sympathetic – of the present position of the German central bank.

Unless there are other suggestions for our agenda, I propose that we now proceed with a discussion of the present world problem of widespread unemployment.

3. Trade Theory and the Problem of Unemployment

Introduced by Paul A. Samuelson

Chairman Cooper: I suggest that we start out with the unemployment problem as the paramount issue for our deliberations, using Bob Solow's Robbins Lecture as background for that problem. Bob, is there anything you want to add to what you said last night?

Robert M. Solow: Not right now.

Cooper: But we can give others an opportunity to comment on what you said. Let us focus first on Europe. Is there anyone who would like to start out with some observations on Europe? Paul:

Paul A. Samuelson: I told Bob in private that if he is to revise his talk, I would suggest that he add a good deal of emphasis to the analysis of what will happen to price levels if a more Keynesian policy is pursued. However, that would be completely relevant to a closed-economy discussion of the unemployment problem, and I want to bring up something peculiarly appropriate for this conference: the international finance and trade aspects of the unemployment problem in Europe. And I want to suggest that if we abandon simple-minded comparative-advantage theory; if we stop prattling that free trade helps everybody all the time, and analyze seriously what dynamic changes in technology do when they're differential to the relative fortunes of different countries, then we may want to consider the hypothesis that the new competition from the Pacific basin in particular – Japan earlier, the 'Four Dragons', and now all the little dragons – may be calling for a market-clearing real wage in Europe which is lower than any previously projected trend would suggest and that some of the difficulties that show up as extra unemployment have this micro aspect.

Now I emphasize this because, although I'm talking about Europe, it has been my analysis since the end of the 1960s that this is what has been happening to the United States, and the slowness of the standard of living of the median American to rise and the change in the pattern of inequality between lousy jobs and good jobs that has arisen is, I think, understandable from dynamic comparative advantage. And I'm just wondering whether it isn't Europe's turn. I'll go further; all revolutions devour their young. Japan is itself taking its place in the queue as Malaysia, Thailand and mainland China begin to occupy the position *vis-à-vis* Japan which Japan occupied earlier *vis-à-vis* the United States. I wish it would become the case that some of the countries of Eastern Europe were breathing hot down the shoulders of Western Europe and the United States, but I see no prospect of that for the next few Claremont conferences.

Cooper: Isn't it an implication of the framework you have in mind that, as the wages of either all workers or most skilled workers are squeezed, some other factor prices ought to be enhanced by the same processes that you're alluding to?

Samuelson: No, I think that the real per capita standard of living of the typical advanced European country, as measured properly by a University of Pennsylvania study, can in toto be diminished in equilibrium by the forces that I'm speaking of. And it's not a zero-sum game in which the non-educated, non-college-going citizens of Europe are losing out to what the educated are gaining, but there's actually either an absolute reduction through time, called for by market-clearing macroeconomics, or a slowdown in the previous customary and to-be-expected rate of increase in the real income per capita of those living in these areas. I could be wrong, but that's what my position is.

Cooper: Let's draw Paul out a little bit. Are you saying that international trade can reduce the real per capita output?

Samuelson: Yes, yes.

Cooper: And could you tell us how that could come about?

Samuelson: Yes; I'll first illustrate with an anecdote. There was in Stockholm in 1991 a gathering of the old-boy clan – I say old boy advisedly because there weren't very many old girls there. It was the ninetieth anniversary of the Nobel awards, and those of us who could dodder arrived, and we all as good soldiers agreed to talk to different Swedish universities. I drew a lot to speak at a business school at the Arctic Circle, and I was taken in a limousine, as I have been many times, on that main highway from Stockholm to the Stockholm airport, where the cream of Swedish manufacturing is to be sampled. It had a slightly tawdry look to it this time, as I remember it, and I thought, well, why not? Really, the Swedish miracle consisted not simply of the fact that, for year after year, there was an 8 percent increase in productivity in Swedish manufacturing, but that it was done in the milieu of a very egalitarian state. That Swedish miracle seemed to have given out by about 1973, and gave out in a way that you really could not, just from the big increase in oil prices, completely understand. And as I drove I thought, well, there is actually nothing that they can do here that can't be done in N parts of the world. I was thinking, of course, of the Pacific basin, but I could also have thought of Puerto Rico and the Mexican border – that Sweden was losing out the monopoly advantage which Swedish factors of production, Swedish labor, had derived from Swedish ingenuity and innovation.

This was my own diagnosis about why there was such a catchup after World War II on the US by the rest of the world, a catchup, by the way, which did not take place for some reason – and that ought to be studied – after World War I. It wasn't that American workers had always been seven feet tall and that foreign workers had been three and a half feet; it wasn't that American workers had diminished in height or that others had increased in height, but that the American initial advantage no longer existed. Textbooks got exported all over the world; students came to our shores. The American multinational corporation has about the same share of world trade and product as it ever did, but it isn't insourced in America; it's outsourced using foreign factors of production. It is fortunate that for many years this didn't require an actual decrease in the mean American standard of living. Indeed, in the age immediately after Keynes, the American real standard of living improved in a fashion that was probably superior to anything in the history of pre-1929 more or less pure American capitalism. But it did show itself in a fall in America's share of the world product, which I suppose was near to 45 percent on VE-day, dropped to 40, to 35, to 30, and now floats somewhere around 22 percent. Now, productivity growth around the world since the early 1970s, for reasons we don't understand, seems to have been at a lower mean rate everywhere; I think there's only one thing that an objective scientist could attribute it to – it's so universal – it's got to be sunspots! [laughter] It has to be extraterrestrial influences because you see it in Japan, you see it everywhere.

Well, I've been telling you anecdotes; now I turn to analysis. Just take the David Ricardo 1817 model of wine and cloth, with Portugal and the US, and add a non-tradable domestic good – bricks – to it, then start stipulating changes in the Ricardian coefficients. Of course you'd only do that in your first year of graduate study, but it's extremely easy to contrive scenarios in which productivity increases everywhere in the world but real income in one part of the world goes down. In fact, it's particularly likely if you use John Stuart Mill's constant-expenditure ratios as your model. That's a model too clever and too easy to handle, and it also gives you some biased results. I'm just suggesting that part of the problem that Bob Solow is talking about in Europe is of this nature.

I've taught in New England for over fifty years, and throughout those years I've seen the same process go on in which industry – whenever manufacturing becomes routine, whenever knowledge mingles and machinery can be transported – will, in a regime of free trade, go to the lower-wage country if productivity in the lower-wage country can successfully imitate that in the other country. International trade and development is like a European bicycle race; I say European bicycle race because we don't know anything about bicycle racing in America, but I'm told that the first fellow has to break the wind for the others, and the big trick is to locate yourself just behind the first fellow. So it's easier to catch up and to imitate than to innovate, but it is still the case, as I read the Penn figures, that the US, despite what Lester Thurow says, has not been surpassed if per capita real output is measured properly.

Cooper: I have on my list Max Corden, Jim Tobin and Bob Mundell, and if they don't cover it, I want to come back to the important issue you raised. I think there's a missing variable up there which we can observe empirically called the terms of trade, and I think to make your case there should be some observables which I think we can observe. But maybe one of the others is going to cover it. Max:

W.M. Corden: Let me pick out some of the issues. David Ricardo [Samuelson] is sitting opposite there. I would hesitate to expound the Law of Comparative Advantage to him, so I hesitate to make some very simple points, many of which I have learned from Paul's writings. The central issue seems to me to what extent the unemployment problem in Europe is caused by external factors. Let's focus our minds on the growth and increasing trade with East Asia; that seems to me the kind of issue that Paul has in mind. Is there some element of a foreign threat or of harm done? Are there adverse Stolper–Samuelson effects from sections of the European Community as a result of the opening up or increased liberalization of trade? Well, in theory there must be, and we can assume that in the recent closing of the textile industry and one or two others, there would be such effects – that equilibrium real wages would have fallen, should have fallen, in Europe and the United States as a result of the Third World and that if there is some degree of real-wage rigidity, we would expect a certain amount of unemployment to be caused by that. What we're left with is an empirical question of how important this is. Everything I've read is that it's probably not a very big element of the total, but there's something there. That's Point One.

The second question is: is there an overall gain or loss from opening up trade? And here, of course, everybody's instinct is on the basis of what I learned originally from Samuelson's *Economics* and other sources: there are going to be gains from trade overall even though there are sectional losses, so there's going to be a Pareto improvement; the gainers can compensate the losers. I can't see that we could have any contrary argument unless there are some very specific distortions in the system whereby there are actual net losses from trade.

And now comes the third factor, and I think it's the one that Dick was hinting at a moment ago. For a given degree of trade restrictions, we ask the question: suppose there is growth in East Asia; would that lead to a net gain or less for other countries, like the United States or Europe? That would involve the Harry Johnson model of whether the growth is biased in an export-substituting or import-substituting direction, with possible effects on the terms of trade. Possibly, to the extent that there is a technology diffusion effect, and foreign countries like Japan get better producing the kinds of products that the United States has been leading in, that would have an adverse terms-of-trade effect in the United States. I can't see the same situation operating in Europe. It's a theoretical possibility, but it doesn't strike me as plausible in practice that the growth of East Asia or, for that matter, the prospective growth of India or China would have an adverse terms-of-trade effect on Europe; I think it's more likely to have a favorable effect.

Samuelson: Mr Moderator, may I raise two hands?

Cooper: Of course.

Samuelson: Very briefly. A predecessor of mine as a *Newsweek* columnist wrote a book called *Economics in One Lesson*. And the right answer to Hazlitt's book happened to my colleague Bob Bishop's mother. She got into a little trouble at an intersection, and a truck driver leaned out the window and said, 'Ma'am, go back for the second lesson'. Now if you learned from me that a change in technology abroad cannot reduce under free trade the total real income of an existing country, then I would really have to say, go back for the second lesson, because what you would learn from me – and it wasn't original with me – is that free trade cannot worsen you in comparison with autarky, but what we are discussing, Max, is the amount of representative consumer surplus from trade, and there is no theorem which says that dynamic developments in technology must lead to no diminution of any country's consumer surplus from trade. Furthermore, what I thought I heard you say – and attributed to Harry Johnson, to whom we can attribute everything, because he has written on everything – isn't an actual negation of your second point, but it's the same point that I'm making. Now if Dick Cooper has a different variation on that, as to why free trade cannot result in a reduction in the market-clearing real wage, the market-clearing real interest rate, the market-clearing real land-rent rate, then I would like to hear it, because I think it's easy to refute.

James Tobin: Well, I was going to try to reconcile what Paul said today with the Stolper–Samuelson argument, but he's already done it. But my argument is a little different. The United States now shares some of the gains from trade with its trading partners. So there is this gain from trade, and part of our real income is due to that gain. But suppose that another United States grows up outside our borders. To make it extreme, suppose that at the end of a dynamic process, they produce everything we do at the same relative prices, so there is no longer an incentive to trade with us. The gains from trade are gone, and our whole population loses from that fact. But during the earlier dynamic process, when that other United States was starting out with low costs and improving all the time, there was all the competition that Paul is talking about, and we were depending on gains from trade that aren't there anymore. This dynamic process over time led to an overall reduction in our real income, and there's no reason why a development of that kind can't result in a reduction of real income in any particular area of the world. What cannot happen is that a country can be made worse off than it would have been as a closed economy.

Samuelson: But that's a very low level.

Tobin: That presumably is a low level. But I'd like to say one more thing. I think what we've been discussing may not have a lot to do with what Bob Solow was talking about last night, because the problem of European unemployment goes back a long time, starting after the first oil shock and intensified by the second oil shock, during which this effect that Paul is talking about was less important.

Cooper: Well, if I can intercede on Paul's behalf, if you think of the process starting in the mid-1950s with Japan – the foreign partner has changed over time – but with Japan, the Four Tigers, and now the Six Sub-Tigers, and so forth, one could in principle resuscitate Paul's argument.

Mundell: I do think that Paul's explanation is going to be very important in the future, so I think we should talk about that, but I think it's going to affect the future more than it has in the past.

I have some figures on the unemployment rates in the OECD countries. I took four years: 1963, 1973, 1983 and 1993. The high unemployment rates in 1963 were for the US, Canada and Ireland, with figures of 5.7, 5.1 and 5.6 percent respectively. All the others were below 4 percent in 1963. In 1973 the picture is little changed: 4.9 percent in the US, 5.5 percent in Canada, with all the European countries below 3 percent. So this is a period of full employment in Europe. But in the 1980s, maybe because of the oil shocks – that's one theory – the picture changes drastically: 10 percent unemployment in the UK, 17 percent in Spain, and so on. In Spain the rise in the unemployment rate over the four decades has been spectacular: in 1963, 1.9 percent; in 1973, 2.5 percent; in 1983, 17 percent; and in 1993, 22 percent.

This sharp increase in European unemployment started with the big economic slump in the early 1980s, and I think it has almost nothing to do with the Asian phenomenon. We need to look for other explanations. I think myself that one explanation is the change all over Europe in social policies which have brought more and more people into the labor force because they get paid for being in the labor force even if they're not working.

Now on the theoretical issue, I understand Paul's model. Instead of going along with the typical textbook case of two countries, take three or more countries, and have some rivalry, with rival producers and complementary producers. Then if one country has a technological advance, that's going to help the complementary countries but it's going to hurt the rival countries. If Kuwait or Iraq expands its production of oil, this is going to hurt all the other oil producers, but it's going to help the other countries. So that clearly is an important part of the model.

But I don't think this is the model that explains the postwar world. I much prefer an earlier Samuelson model, a Heckscher–Ohlin-based model. Remember 1948, when Samuelson's articles came out on factor-price equalization. Students read them and we read them, but you looked around the world, and the articles didn't seem to be very relevant, because factor prices in Japan were a tenth, and in Europe were a quarter or a third or half of what they were in the United States. And you would have said that the model isn't very good. But if you move ahead to the 1980s, suddenly after thirty years that model looks great, because a very important degree of factor-price equalization has been achieved in the OECD area. Contributing to that, of course, has been a big movement toward free trade, but we've also had capital movements, we've had sharing of technology and we've had this catchup phenomenon. When you use the Heckscher–Ohlin model, which I think is a step above the Ricardian model, you find that certain factors of production may be hurt by trade, and it may be that as a result of the trade that has opened up between the United States and Europe that labor in the United States didn't gain as much as it would have gained had this catchup situation not occurred. But I think the country as a whole has gained.

Samuelson: Let me just call attention to the basic fact that has been established by ten University of Pennsylvania studies over a long period of time. What they show is a massive increase in per capita real income in Europe, in the Pacific basin, and in country after country. And so what's going on here is more than a Heckscher–Ohlin reallocation between factors of production within countries; there is a differential between regions, and I don't think it's explicable in a strict Heckscher–Ohlin theory. The production functions are the same all over the world, and have always been the same, including the differential behavior of knowledge and the passage of knowledge. We used to be taught that rubber was produced exclusively in South America. It was a crime, a punishable crime, to remove one sapling of a rubber tree to anywhere else in the world. But one sapling is very hard to control, and it moved to Malaysia, so the whole industry moved. Well, knowledge is like that. MIT has opened doors, and foreigners have been coming in for years in a way that they did not do after World War I.

Solow: I want to come back to the unemployment question rather than the overall gains-from-trade issue. It obviously doesn't take anything very fancy to suggest that if the relevant world, the relevant trading world, suddenly becomes enlarged to include China, Indonesia, Brazil and so on, that relevant trading world will have experienced an overall increase in its labor/capital ratio, its labor/other-factor ratio. And it's natural then to imagine that the real wage around the world is likely to fall compared with what it otherwise would have been. It doesn't require complete factor-price equalization to make that point. So it nags everyone that this may be the important thing that's happening, and as Max pointed out, if you add to that any amount of real-wage rigidity in the advanced countries, then it's perfectly natural to imagine that the outcome might be an increase in unemployment in those countries.

That this can happen, and to some extent probably does happen, I think is intuitive to all of us. The question then arises of how important, quantitatively, that is, and there I have to say that most of the research that has been done suggests that it's not the major explanation. I just happen to have read a paper by Dick Friedman and a paper by Gary Berkowitz directed essentially at this question. First of all, the timing is wrong. So far as the US is concerned, the deterioration of the relative position of unskilled labor began before it could have been primarily a response to import competition from poor countries. Secondly, if you look at industry by industry in the short run and ask whether these things happen first in industries which are most subject to that kind of competition, the answer turns out to be no. So I think the conclusion that one has to come to, both from theory and from what empirical research there has been, is that in principle this is surely a possibility, a possible contributor to the increased average level of unemployment in Europe and in North America, but that it is hard to make a case that the drastic numbers that I read out last night and that Bob Mundell described a minute ago, are primarily a reflection of this sort of import competition.

Cooper: If I could add to what Bob Solow has just said, it's important to appreciate that Paul Samuelson's model requires the intermediating variable of relative price changes. That's critical, and we can actually get some observations on the things you need in order to do the kind of studies that Bob is referring to. A study that he didn't mention has been done by my colleague, Robert Lawrence, focusing on the United States, so it does not directly address the question in Europe. He looked very carefully at whether one can explain the clearly observable, and to many people troubling, growth in dispersion of the US wage structure over the last fifteen years, with the wages of unskilled workers, depending on how you define them, actually falling and the compensation of higher-skilled employees rising substantially. So we've had a dramatic increase in the dispersion of wages in the United States, and he posed the question to what extent this can be attributed to international competition – in particular, competition coming from low-wage countries. And it turns out, as Bob Solow has just said but also according to this study, that very little of what we observe can be attributed to foreign trade. The reason is that the mediating variables – namely, relative prices – don't move in the right direction for the theory. They just don't support the theory, and that leads Lawrence to conclude – which in a way is a cop-out, but this doesn't make it wrong – that what is really driving the situation is technical change of some kind – that various biases in technology are driving the change in wage dispersion. Then, assuming that the same technological drivers are taking place all around the world, if Europe has greater wage rigidity than the United States, the phenomenon shows up in the United States as greater dispersion of wages and in Europe as higher unemployment – all without any reference to trade.

Morris: Just on Bob Lawrence's work, because I think it's very germane to this discussion, he has written an excellent piece for my journal in which he concluded that, along with the technological change, US productivity in services has plummeted during this period. And this gets us back to all sorts of things we're talking about on the social front. But that one can measure the decline in the productivity in services, however amorphous that is, I find very interesting.

Johnson: Well, Dick, I thought you might like a European point of view. I'm one of two Europeans here. Britain, as you all know, is part of Europe, although some people back at home sometimes tend to forget it, but I'm speaking myself as a European. I'd like to start off by making a point which I think is often overlooked about the 'Tigers' – about countries like South Korea and Taiwan. I think there is actually a paradox here. And the paradox is, why are they not doing even better in international competition than they are? They are, in fact, not doing all that well. They are able to import all the latest technological equipment that we can sell them. Their labor forces are in some cases better educated than our own, and yet their productivity levels are one-third of those in the United States and about two-fifths of the average in Europe. I think one is forced to conclude that there is a missing element in a lot of our models. You can combine the labor and the capital factors of production as conventionally understood, and yet you don't get at all the same result in different countries. I think we have to look at what's sometimes called the X factor, the management factor, in which undoubtedly American and, in many cases, European industrial organization still have a comparative advantage, especially in more advanced industrial sectors which involve more than merely assembling components with screwdrivers. In a way, we've been blessedly protected from the kind of competitiveness which these countries could have achieved had they got their act together on the management front. This takes a little longer. It will of course happen over time, and then inevitably their real incomes will rise to the kind of level that we have; the real income in Singapore is already as high as it is in Britain. And then, of course, their exchange rates will go up.

This brings me to my second point, which has been alluded to in terms of relative prices, competitiveness and the terms of trade, but I really think we have to look at what exchange rates do. It's been implicitly said by several people that exchange rates don't in fact move in order to equalize unit labor costs; in other words, they do not move in such a way that relative income per head is an exact reflection of relative productivity per head. But the exchange-rate movements that we've had have in fact gone some way to solving these competitiveness problems. If you look at United States competitiveness by most measures, the fall in the dollar since 1985 has changed America from being something like one-third less competitive than most other countries to about one-third more competitive. This may be partly responsible for the failure of real income per head to rise in America. Indeed, it's higher in Europe than it is in America now, although our productivity is still some way behind yours. In the European exchange-rate mechanism [ERM], the net result of the two so-called crises we've had in the last two years has been that Europe itself has become 15 percent more competitive against its main trading partners: America, Japan and the Tigers. So while exchange rates never move in an orderly and disciplined manner in spite of all our best efforts, very often they do move in the broad sense required, and they do solve some of these intractable problems of competitiveness.

I think we still do have a problem in Europe in that the gains in competitiveness have been rather unevenly distributed. They've gone to countries which have left the ERM or have devalued, such as Britain, Italy and Spain. And you have countries like Germany and France which are still uncompetitive, or not as competitive as they should be by European or by world standards, because of the fact that their income levels per head are still higher in terms of purchasing-power-parity exchange rates than American levels, yet their productivity is still somewhat lower than in the United States. Therefore I would acknowledge the fact that there has to be some kind of real-income adjustment in Europe relative to the rest of the world.

But I would just like to nail one frequent delusion, which is that somehow Europe has made itself uncompetitive by having much higher non-wage labor costs than the United States. This is not true. In both cases, non-wage labor costs are about 30 percent of direct pay. The problem is that some countries in Europe pay more than the average in terms of social protection and non-wage labor costs – notably Italy, Germany and France – while some are way below average, and indeed way below the United States, such as the United Kingdom.

So just to conclude, I would say that we ought to look at exchange-rate movements as being part of the solution to competitiveness problems. If we could control exchange rates better, as indeed we are trying to do in Europe, then we might be able to achieve some kind of real exchange-rate equilibrium – some kind of constant competitiveness lodestar for external policy. This will, I think, be even more difficult in relations between Europe and the United States and Japan and the Tigers, but it could still happen of its own accord even if we don't know how to make it happen.

Samuelson: Well, the Devil has to quote scripture for his purposes. It's difficult to discuss rationally whether somebody who has done very well has perhaps not done as well as he might have been expected to do. But let's just take the actual Penn studies of what's happened to the Four Dragons and let's compare their meteoric rise *vis-à-vis* Western Europe and the United States with anything that was observed in history within Western Europe, such as the rise of Germany in the nineteenth century *vis-à-vis* England. I do not see why anyone can say that Taiwan, which started from about the same level as mainland China a few years ago, and then reached levels eighteen times the per capita real income of mainland China, or Singapore which went from 9 percent of US GDP per capita to 35 percent, ought to have done better and ought to have been expected to do better. Now it could be a meaningful hypothesis – let's wait a long time – to see whether these particular countries, because of some presumed inherited deficiency in management, are going to level off at a level inferior to the Western European pattern. I'm not sure that I would like to bet on their odds, because I don't see what the evidence has been in the actual time series.

Johnson: Could I just have a quick two-handed reply to that, which is that I think it very commonly happens that people look at productivity changes and not at productivity levels. If you start at a productivity level close to zero, you can get very dramatic year-to-year gains in productivity and yet your productivity level is still very low by international standards. And that, incidentally, has been one of the problems of assessing Mrs Thatcher's so-called revolution in Britain. We got some quite impressive productivity changes, higher than in partner countries, and yet, because we started from way back, we are just a little less way back than we were.

Corden: Let me come back to the central issue that Bob Mundell started us up on. I'd like to focus on the future rather than the past for a moment, and draw attention to a possible big problem and a possible solution. It looks as if the major developing countries are going to be opening up and growing very fast in the next ten or fifteen years. India has begun a big liberalization process or is just on the verge of it, and has tremendous possibilities of becoming an exporter of low-skilled labor products. Brazil has yet to really make the impact it could. Now these are the two biggest developing countries outside the former socialist bloc. And then, of course, there's China. Now the developed world could respond by protection, could simply refuse to take the goods and cut itself off from this, but let's assume for a moment that to a considerable extent we will get this big boom. Well, certainly one would then expect a major Stolper–Samuelson effect in the developed world, everywhere in the world, including Japan – a big decline in the equilibrium real wage of the very lowest-skilled people. We've already begun to see this, and it's going to get worse. And that will manifest itself as unemployment, because when you get to a certain level of equilibrium real wages – below the minimum that people will accept in relation to unemployment benefits and so on – this, it looks to me, could be a very big problem.

If I ask myself whether there is a positive side to this situation, well, the positive side is that as our countries, the developed countries, keep on growing, presumably the demand for services will go up. And taking into account the demographic changes – the growth of the aged population – I can visualize a big counteracting effect, a big growth in demand for low-skilled people. It's the same kind of people who will no longer be working in the clothing and textile industry; they will be working in old people's homes. So we have to consider the balance of these considerations, and I think it would be worth reflecting on this if you want to look ahead.

Solomon: I have one macro point on the general issue of the relationship between what's going on in East Asia and unemployment in Europe – a point that hasn't been mentioned yet. This unemployment, which goes back a long way, has gotten much worse just in the last three or four years during the recession, particularly on the Continent. And it just so happens that during this period, East Asian countries in particular and developing countries in general have moved into large current-account deficits. It has been a big change in their balance of payments, and at the same time the current-account deficit of the OECD countries has gone down by a very large amount. So you've had a demand impact from the developing countries which should have worked to reduce a portion of the unemployment that Bob Solow talked about last night. When I looked at the figures recently, I was surprised by the very large movement in payments imbalances in the last three or four years.

Cooper: But doesn't that, at least in part, reflect the recession in the United States and subsequently in Japan and Europe?

Solomon: If we did a set of cyclically adjusted balances of payments we'd still find a large movement.

Johnson: A two-handed question for Bob. Does not that reflect the role of the developing countries as capital importers? They have no difficulty in attracting private capital; they always need a current-account deficit.

Solomon: It's related to the enormous increase in capital mobility that has occurred. That's a subject we may want to get to.

Cooper: Lionel McKenzie is concerned about the looseness of some of the concepts we have been using, so he is now going to straighten us out.

Lionel W. McKenzie: As an empiricist, it's natural for me to bring these questions up. I mentioned last night that I was worried about unemployment, what was being measured when we measure unemployment, and how these measures might differ between different countries and, I should have added, between different times. But I also want to raise questions about our measurement of standards of living and per capita gross national product. People have been speaking as if they were absolutely sure of what's been happening with these things. In his presidential address for the American Economic Association recently, Zvi Griliches said that there has not been a decline in the rate of US technological progress; it was purely a matter of a shift in the composition of output. In those areas where it's not too difficult, perhaps, to measure technological progress – although there are problems because of the great difficulty resulting from changes in quality – in those areas there has not been a decline in technological progress, but actually an acceleration.

If you move from technological progress to how the standard of living has changed, it seems to me elementary that you must take account of the enormous sums that have been spent both privately and publicly to improve the environment. I think our environment has, in fact, been improved considerably as a result of these expenditures, so to count those expenditures as being without product, it seems to me, is quite inappropriate. To have a fair judgment of whether the rate of increase in our standard of living has gone down, we would have to take full account of these changes, and I'm not at all sure that we do. I don't want to ask you to stop referring to these concepts, but to do it with some degree of modesty.

4. Unemployment and Monetary Policy

Introduced by Robert M. Solow

Chairman Cooper: Perhaps Bob Solow would be willing now to be a little more fulsome than he was last night about what, if he were in charge of Europe, he would actually do about the problem of unemployment. He gave some hints, but he didn't actually give a prescription.

Solow: Well, I had more than my share of time last night, but I will just amplify a little and say that I meant what I said. It seems to me that there is room in most of Europe – most especially in France, Belgium, Denmark, the Netherlands and Britain – for demand expansion and that there is sitting there an unknown set of percentage points of unemployment, perhaps 3 or 4 or even 5 percent, that could safely be eliminated that way. By safely I mean with very little acceleration of inflation above the currently very low level. Fiscal policy appears to be paralyzed in Europe, in part for good reasons. Dick mentioned that this is not the case in Germany and France, and I think that's right. But in any case, rather than start that debate, it seems to me that the obvious way to start a policy of, if possible, coordinated expansion of aggregate demand is on the monetary policy side. More than that I don't think I want to say right now.

Johnson: I wonder if I could reply to that, because there are a lot of countries in Europe which have wanted to loosen monetary policy. Britain and Italy have been able to do so only by leaving the exchange-rate mechanism, which has certainly brought short-term benefits to their economies. Britain is now in the second year of moderately strong economic recovery. The main

problem is for countries which have linked their exchange rates
and thus their interest rates to those of Germany, although one
must say that Germany has not got the biggest unemployment
problem, except in the east. So for Germany it's in a sense less
urgent to cut interest rates. Nevertheless, Germany has done so,
and the other countries that stayed in the system have had quite a
substantial loosening of monetary policy.

I'm not sure that Bob Solow has allowed sufficiently for the
time lags before the cut in interest rates feeds through to the
whole of the economy. There is a danger that many people are
conscious of, not only in the Bundesbank, that if we continue to
cut interest rates too quickly, if we sort of panic that we haven't
done enough, we will turn out to have done too much. And we
shall only know that in a couple of years. By then it will be too
late to reverse the engines. In most of the forecasts, the European countries are seen as recovering some time this year or as
late as next year, so that by 1996 or '97 you could have quite a
strong European-wide recovery. I think that's why European
countries are now looking more to what I know Bob does not
like to call structural changes, but anyway let's call them changes
in labor-market institutions. And while we in Britain, for example, are quite virtuous in having deregulated our labor market, I
think we score rather badly in – I won't call it incomes policy,
because that has an old-fashioned statutory flavor, but policies
designed in some way to control the growth of real incomes.
Some European countries – Belgium, Spain, Italy – are able to
have national negotiations in which employers and unions voluntarily agree to have a lower nominal wage increase than
otherwise, which they hope means no sacrifice in real-wage
terms. In Britain and in some other countries, it has actually
been quite difficult to have any kind of nation-wide wage agree-
ments, and we therefore have to find some other way of moder-
ating wage increases other than having high unemployment.
And that is the whole paradox of unemployment; people are
afraid to move too fast to reduce it in case it's a condition for
restraining wage and price increases. I'm not sure that this
consideration is as important as it used to be in keeping infla-

tion down, but it is still a constraint on government's policy behavior.

Solow: Excuse me, Dick, I just want to make one or two further remarks. I'm going to leave it to Jim Tobin or someone else to comment on those very long lags in monetary policy which seem always to be longer in one direction than in the other and highly variable whenever that is convenient. I do want to say that part of the burden of what I was trying to say last night is that I think the notion that, oh, well, the European economies are recovering, and some time toward the end of 1995 or early 1996 things will be much better – I think that is an inadequate response. The true labor-market problem, it seems to me, is that in European conditions, two more years of high unemployment will make it very, very difficult ever – well, not ever, but in politically and socially meaningful time spans – to get the unemployment rate down. It is not harmless to allow 10 or 11 percent unemployment to persist for an extra two years simply in order to allow things to happen in the most orderly way.

Cooper: Just so we are starting from a common factual base, let me indicate, as a crude measure of monetary conditions, roughly where short-term nominal interest rates – money-market rates – are now: 2 percent in Japan, 3 percent in the United States, 5 percent in the Netherlands and Britain, 6 percent in Germany and France, 8 percent in Italy. If one tries to get an empirical handle on real interest rates, the core inflation rate in most of the continental countries is now around 2 or $2^1/2$ percent, so we're talking about real short-term interest rates in major European countries of 3 to 4 percent at a time when economies are slack both in terms of capacity utilization and in terms of unemployment.

Thomas D. Willett: I'd like to start by saying that I share very strongly Bob Solow's concern with the high unemployment rates in Europe, both for the human cost in its own right and for the feedback effects on trade policies – in particular, the contribution that unemployment may make to trade barriers against Eastern Europe and the emerging market economies. So I think from several perspectives, this is quite a problem.

I was quite surprised a couple of months ago when Sven Arndt and I were at a conference in Vienna, sponsored by the Institute for International Economics, that probably 90 percent of the economists there from all over Europe were taking predominantly the supply-side view of unemployment that Bob Solow was arguing against as being the complete explanation. I have been reading articles on supply side versus demand side, and for every article that purported to find conclusions one way or the other, I would the next month find another article that contradicted it. If I remember correctly, Bob in his lecture last night alluded to the research literature on this subject as not being in very satisfactory shape. I would ask Bob for characterization of the kinds or research studies we should be trying to do. We have a number of dissertation students sitting here as observers who are looking for topics, so any ideas about policy research that we should be doing on this issue would be very welcome.

Solow: I don't want to let the students here go away unsatisfied; they're more important than we are. Let me just say that the mine that needs to be explored on these labor-market questions has to do with the availability in the US and in some European countries of gross-flow data. Instead of looking just at net changes in employment and unemployment, actually look at gross flows from unemployment to employment, from unemployment to out of the labor force, from employment to unemployment, from employment to out of the labor force, and so on. It is even possible to look a little bit at exit probabilities from unemployment according to the duration of a preceding spell of unemployment, and things of that sort. These are the areas where I think research is needed, is possible, and will pay off.

Solomon: I have taken a look at the unemployment problem in Europe, independently of Bob Solow, and had come to a very similar conclusion before last night. I want to say a few words in support of his conclusion and carry it a bit further. One bit of evidence: it comes from the OECD, which measures output gaps in Europe. The latest OECD economic survey shows substantial unused capacity. Now that doesn't answer the question whether European firms are willing to take people on at the existing wage cost. But the existence of unused capacity, I think, has some relevance to the policy issue we are discussing.

My second observation has to do with Herbert Giersch, the German economist. In the first half of the 1980s, he talked about Europe's sclerosis, and told the world that Germany couldn't possibly have a higher growth rate, for reasons very similar to those that Bob expounded last night. Well, when unification came along, Germany had a big dose of increased aggregate demand, and employment and output certainly grew more rapidly. True, inflation picked up in Germany at the same time. One could argue that if the Germans had been willing and able to let the Deutsche Mark go up at the time of unification, they would have had less inflation.

The third point I want to make is that, assuming there is scope for increased demand to reduce unemployment, I'm not sure that it has be solely through monetary policy. Yes, as Bob said last night and as I think I said in the question I asked him, we recognize that budget deficits are high. Nevertheless, I'm not sure they're so high that you couldn't get some temporary – temporary – fiscal stimulus in some of the European countries. France, in particular, has a structural budget deficit of about 3 percent of GDP, which is not outstandingly large. I don't suppose anybody would expect Germany to undertake fiscal stimulus, but maybe some of the other countries that we've been talking about could, at least on a temporary basis.

Mundell: I don't disagree completely with Professor Solow, but I think he's about 25 percent correct about the scope for expansionary policies of the Keynesian type. There is some scope for expansionary monetary and fiscal policies, but that depends upon the condition of the budget deficit, the size of the public debt, the degree of confidence in the exchange rate, and the nature of the problem. These high unemployment rates of 8, 9, 10, 11, 12 percent in Europe have gone on for twelve years. This is not a Keynesian cyclical problem; it's a phenomenon that has persisted over a long period of time. And over that period, Europe has experienced depreciating currencies in the first half of the 1980s, followed by a period of appreciating currencies and, since the exchange crises of the early 1990s, by a period of more or less stable currencies.

Now when you think about expansionary fiscal policies applied, let's say, to the case of Italy, that country left the ERM in September 1992, when the dollar was about 1,100 lire. Since then the lira has depreciated to something like 1,700, monetary policy has eased up, and interest rates have come down, so there has been a very definite expansion in policy. But as far as the fiscal position is concerned, there is no possibility of fiscal expansion when the Italian budget deficit is something like 10 percent of GDP and when the public debt is 105 percent of GDP. If the public debt were exactly 100 percent of GDP and if the interest rate were 11 percent, then 11 percent of GDP would have to be paid out by the government in the form of interest payments. Of course the Italians have gained a bit because of a fall in interest rates. But if Italy expands further on the fiscal side, it will create a crisis of confidence, and no one is going to want to hold public debt. If the Italians expand monetary policy more rapidly than they have been, they won't be able to finance the public debt by selling bonds. Much of the Italian public debt has been bought by Italians, but if there is a crisis of confidence in the bond market, there would be the risk of a very substantial further depreciation of the lira. This would create havoc, and it would not be possible to continue it.

Prior to 1971, Italy had for many years maintained a fixed exchange rate – 625 lire to the dollar. And then, after August 15, 1971, Governor Carli let the lira float along with the other European currencies. At first the lira appreciated; the dollar went down to 585. The Italians thought this was a great thing. I talked to Carli the day after this occurred, and I said that it seemed strange to let the lira appreciate, because Italy wasn't strong enough to maintain the appreciation. He said, 'You're right, Mundell, but we have to appreciate against the dollar for the sake of European solidarity'. Well, the appreciation lasted for a few months; then, throughout the 1970s and early 1980s, the lira depreciated. By 1985 it was down to 2,200 lire to the dollar. When Italy moved into the ERM, it finally got some monetary discipline, but it has not yet achieved fiscal discipline. I think it would be a mistake to tell the Italians to do anything other than what they're doing; they can't afford additional fiscal expansion.

I divide Italy into three parts. Roughly speaking, in northern Italy, male unemployment is 4 percent, female unemployment, 8 percent; in central Italy, male unemployment is 8 percent, female unemployment, 16 percent; and in southern Italy, male unemployment is 16 percent, female unemployment, 32 percent. Now it isn't quite as neat as that. The Bank of Italy didn't print those figures. But nothing on the demand side is going to change the unemployment rate in southern Italy; the attempt throughout the 1970s and 1980s to reduce the high female unemployment rate there by monetary and fiscal policies didn't work. Bob Solomon mentioned the possibility of monetary and fiscal expansion in Germany as a result of acquiring another country and 18 million people. But the German case was unique in that when unification occurred, the public debt was something like 40 percent of GDP and the budget was in approximate balance. And Germany had a currency that everyone had confidence in. But even Germany can't expand much without running the risk that people are going to stop investing there, that interest rates are going to rise, and that the bond market is going to crack. Germany has been in the best position to expand, and it already has done the expansion, but there's no other country in Europe that's in a position to do that, so I don't think that fiscal or monetary expansion will really work or make much of a dent in this very substantial and enduring unemployment. I think that we're forced to attack the problem by looking at the supply-side factors that have been the cause of the unemployment.

Johnson: Dick, let me do a two-hander on that because I did want to pick up Bob Mundell's point on bond rates in Europe. This is an often neglected aspect of monetary policy. Europe's conservative policies on both budget deficits and short-term interest rates have in fact succeeded in lowering long-term interest rates to below those in the United States for the key countries we're talking about with high unemployment. In France, for example, long-bond rates are $5^{1}/_{2}$ percent. Even in Britain, our long-bond rate is no more than 6$^{1}/_{2}$ percent. Now that should be a launching pad for an investment boom, particularly because in some countries, such as Germany and France, long-term industrial finance counts for more than short-term finance, which tends to dominate in the UK. So I think you have to give Europe credit for having lowered inflationary expectations to the point where long-bond rates can be quite low even in nominal terms. In real terms we're still talking about 2$^{1}/_{2}$ to 3$^{1}/_{2}$ percent, which is a fairly good long-run interest rate if you're expecting to have real economic growth of that order of magnitude.

Cooper: Picking up something Bob Mundell said, let me just observe that the nice thing about economics is that most things are not either/or, but they can be quantified. We should constantly keep that in mind. Bob Solow did not say last night that there was no supply-side unemployment; he just said that there was some demand-side unemployment. And he ventured that the ratio was 60:40 – 60 percent supply side and 40 percent demand side. Bob Mundell gave him 25 percent of his argument, and I wasn't sure whether Bob meant by that 25 percent of the total unemployment or 25 percent of the 40 percent, which would be 10 percent of the unemployment. I would add a third possibility – that some of this measured unemployment represents people who are actually employed but collecting unemployment compensation. That I know to be the case in Spain and Italy; to what extent it is true in the northern countries is more problematic. This possibility probably can't explain more than 10 percent of the unemployment – which, however, in Spain would mean 2, 3 or even 4 percentage points of the high measured Spanish unemployment.

Tobin: Well, with respect to what Dick Cooper has just said, I believe Bob Solow had in mind one other major kind of unemployment – namely, the possibility that if you run the economy with tight macro policy for a long time and have high amounts of Keynesian demand-side unemployment, maybe you will have a self-fulfilling prophecy, converting the demand-side unemployment into unemployable people either by their attitudes toward work, their use of social insurance, or their lack of experience and skill. I think there is a prospect that if the central banks and governments running European countries keep on the way they've been going for the last fifteen years, perhaps by the year 2000 they will tell us that what may have grown to 20 percent unemployment is all structural. And maybe they will have succeeded in making it that way. I think that is one of the reasons why Solow has emphasized that something ought to be done about this policy soon, rather than cautiously and later. I'm inclined to out-Solow Solow and think he was being unduly cautious in his classification of unemployment as 60 percent supply side and 40 percent demand side. I think the European governments are guilty of having run unduly restrictive macro policies – whether monetary, fiscal or both – for a long, long time, maybe beginning with the first oil shock and never really recovering from the two big recessions of the 1970s and the early 1980s. Then their sights got low, and what people talk about as recovery is just the limited movement up from a deep recession rather than recovery to ground that is forever lost.

If I may comment on one cyclical regularity in the history of policy – namely, that whenever there is a business-cycle downturn and a rise in unemployment rates, there is a boom in theories of structural unemployment. It's a sort of denial syndrome that the unemployment can be remedied by increasing government spending or by lowering taxes. People seem to have an appetite for cataclysmic theories about what's going on. I'm old enough to remember hearing this in the Great Depression – exactly the same thing that I heard from a professor of law on TV the other day – that we can no longer distribute income and get jobs through labor markets; we've got to find some other way to do it because human labor is becoming obsolete and is just not needed anymore. Bob Solow and I encountered this in the early 1960s. There were books on the left and William McChesney Martin on the right, who believed that a proper definition of full employment would imply an unemployment rate of 7 percent instead of 4 percent, or something like that. And now we have it again; it always comes up.

One thing to look at in explaining unemployment is whether there is an unfavorable shift in what we call the Beveridge Curve

– the relationship between unemployment and vacancies – so that labor markets aren't working as well in the sense that at any one time there are both more vacancies and more unemployment than there was before. That's not what is happening now. If you look at vacancies in Europe compared with unemployment, it's not that there are a lot of jobs that aren't being taken by the workers available because they're not qualified or because the jobs are located in the wrong places. Vacancies are negligible, and so there is a more traditional Keynesian explanation of what has happened – namely, that in the job market there is both less demand as expressed in the availability of jobs and greater supply as expressed in unemployment. It's also true in the United States, by the way, that there are many fewer vacancies in the help-wanted ads than one would expect at the rates of unemployment we have now. So the labor market is weaker than it looks just by using the labor-supply side of the equation. That's another topic to add to Bob Solow's counsel to potential scholars who want to work on such things.

Now a big problem we have is that the attitude of European governments and central banks that make fiscal and monetary policy is imported – maybe they're not aware of this – from the new classical macroeconomics in the United States. I'm referring to the supreme confidence in the self-adjustment capability of the economy, so that it can adjust to any shock just as well without explicit macro policy as with it – that holding the line on inflation will not do any harm in the medium run or even in the short run because the economy will adapt to an exchange rate that's fixed or to a tight M1 policy as well as it will adapt to anything else. That's a theoretical proposition that I don't think many economists in Europe believe, but certainly policy is made on that assumption. If we take the London *Economist* as a sample of establishment views, I've never seen it advocate or accept in recent years any expansionary move in either monetary or fiscal policy.

This policy stance has failed. The G–7 has failed. They get together and they talk about coordinating macro policy just a little bit around the edges, and they don't face this very large problem. I remember when the OECD governments in the 1960s were so bold as to vote for a real growth target of 5 percent per year for that decade. And they actually achieved that target. I can't imagine the G–7 doing anything but talking about financial stability.

Samuelson: I want to start out with a proposition by George Bernard Shaw: 'Never strike a child except in anger'. Well, it's in that noble spirit that I want to confess to some wholesome paranoia against the Treaty of Maastricht and against the current revival of so-called independent central banking. These two topics are actually interconnected. For example, the Bank of France is about to be given its independence. I said to a French colleague, 'There's been, I presume, a spirited debate about the evils of the Ministry of Finance's control of the central bank and how it uses its printing-press power to create inflation'. He replied, 'Oh, not at all, no debate at all; the central bank independence is required by the Treaty of Maastricht'. There's a whole list of things that you have to do if you're to be kosher and a particular set of dates by which these things are to take place.

Now whenever I say something critical about the Treaty of Maastricht, people say, 'Oh, you don't believe in the division of labor and the great changes in Europe'. And my sincere answer is quite the contrary: I think that the European Common Market has been one of the great developments of our time and that the improved division of labor and the huge market that's been created have been for Europe and for the world of central importance. But somehow to confuse that with a timetable of when there is to be one central bank in Europe with a system of narrowly pegged exchange rates is in my mind to commit a logical misdemeanor and an empirical felony.

Let's take some recent problems in Europe, and I will actually broaden it a bit to include Japan, because Japan in my mind has always been an island off one of the coasts of Europe. The Germans, I think, have had some serious problems with their reunification. Those problems were exacerbated by a botched program, and I've not been as critical of the Bundesbank in recent years as I have been in the past because of those genuine problems. Turning to the UK and Italy, they were forced out of the exchange-rate arrangement; as is said in Europe, they were forced out by speculators. Well, the Lord works in wonderful ways His great things to accomplish. Maggots are used by the Lord to cure wounds; that's part of His grand system. And speculators are the maggots who are used by the Lord to get rid of the worst aspects of exchange-rate problems. Instead of Italy having to be regretful and instead of the UK being punished by a vengeful Lord, the two countries have actually done a little bit better with their freedom. Now we mustn't make too much of that, because it's always easier to do a little better at the beginning of these depreciations. But something is forgotten when people are blissfully confident that a pegged exchange-rate system in Europe would work well in the steady state. A pegged Bretton Woods system worked fine when the American dollar was grossly undervalued for a long period of time and the American people had spare cash, but the adjustments which needed to be made – and which did not get made – led to the breakdown.

Now let me speak about independent central banks, because not enough has been said about them. Under Maastricht, any central banks not under the thumb of government would become independent. If we became part of Europe, the Federal Reserve, which has a doubtful and shadowy independence under our present system, would have to become completely independent. I've quoted George Bernard Shaw; on central banks and central bankers, I have to quote another great economic authority, Napoleon Bonaparte, who said that you should hang an occasional general just to encourage the others. That's how I feel about central bankers. I don't think that John Crow is the worst central banker Canada ever had, but he presided over a period of time in which Canadian unemployment went up to 11 percent. He professed that he was going to follow the same exact rule of every central banker – I've been looking for an exception – namely, to guard the stability of the price level. I always look for them to say, 'Yes, and real output is also one of our goals'. They sometimes finesse this by saying, 'We are really doing that job when we are taking care of the price level', because somehow – I guess by a new classical economics which they never learned in school – real growth is going to happen.

The most recent case is the celebration of the one hundredth anniversary of the Bank of Italy. I was invited to attend; I didn't have that kind of spare time or that kind of spare cash, but Governor Fazio sent me his speech and Paul Volcker's speech. It was a much better than average Paul Volcker speech. He explained why central banks could be independent. He said it's anomalous to give a group of people in a society where there are three estates – the legislature, the judiciary and the executive – a fourth estate. But, he explained, we don't really do that. What we give the central bankers is temporary, day-to-day autonomy. They're always on a string, and what is given can be taken away. Well, that's my version of the Napoleonic doctrine. But Paul Volcker, who in my book deserves the highest grades of recent central banking history – and recent goes back a long way – to Miller, to Burns, to Martin, to ...

Paul W. McCracken: To Eccles?

Samuelson: No, I don't want to form that difficult judgment. Hard cases make bad law, and I'm trying to avoid that. But there was not one single sentence in this well thought-out speech by Paul Volcker which said that the central bank has any responsibility for the real output of the economy. Now I submit that Paul Volcker in office made a liar out of Paul Volcker giving a speech over chicken *à la* king. Paul Volcker in the summer of 1982, seeing that the recession was deeper and lasting longer than before, and weighing carefully the window of opportunity and the risks of inflation, deliberately took on an expansionary policy which focused on economic recovery rather than exclusive concern for guarding the price level. In some degree risky, it was a magnificent decision. Far from what the gnomes of Zurich predicted – by the way, the gnomes of Zurich all live in New York –

Cooper: Except those who live in London.

Samuelson: Far from what the gnomes predicted, the bond market went up. Soon – actually too soon from the standpoint of basic economic logic – the stock market took its cue from the bond market, and by November 1982 all talk about 'you can pull on a string but you can't push a string' was completely forgotten, and properly so, because it was negated by experience. And the economy made a healthy recovery. It was the American locomotive – the only locomotive – that operated in the world economy. Main Street in America felt it, Main Street in Japan felt it, and all of this was accompanied by sharply reduced US inflation.

Now that's the kind of behavior which every rational central bank, if given its autonomy on a limited day-to-day basis, ought to be taking into account. They should never think solely of the goodies of the jobs that can be created in the next eighteen months if, in some degree, that's going to jeopardize price-level behavior and cause them to have to do the things which are going to take away jobs thirty-six months from now. The Bundesbank is given as an example, because apparently its charter says that it has only one goal: the protection of the currency.

Cooper: It is true that the basic statute of the Bundesbank enjoins the Bundesbank to pursue stability of the mark. It is also true, however, that the same statute enjoins the Bundesbank to cooperate with the government in the pursuit of overall economic policy. The central bankers over the years have kept reiterating the first of those injunctions but not the second, and of course most of the rest of us have taken our knowledge of the central bank statute from those speeches. And this is a case where repetition slowly transforms into revealed truth.

Samuelson: Well, the president of the Cleveland Federal Reserve Bank, who testified with me before the Joint Economic Committee, justified why a person like himself, who is not approved by any political body, should be allowed to help shape policy. He said, 'I should not be allowed to do so unless I swear to the oath that the only thing I'm going to consider is what I learned in the UCLA classroom – namely, that the sanctity of the price level is the only thing I should ever look on'. This point of view is in the ascendancy at the present time, so when Governor Crow in Canada wasn't reappointed, I rejoiced a little. I must say for Governor Fazio, that reading his text with the microscope that I used on Paul Volcker's text, it was a better text. He did have considerations with respect to real output.

But part of the problem in Europe is that the psychology I have described is rampant. I never thought I would live to see the day when a Swedish central bank would raise the interest rate to 500 percent a very short time in order to do what? In order to look the mark in the eye and be a good supplicant to get into the Common Market. Of course it cost a lot of money; it cost the Swedish economy its strength, and in three weeks the policy was abandoned. Professor Vandermeulen asked about the mystery of how a Sweden, operating at a 2 percent unemployment rate for forty years, could suddenly have 9 percent. That's because economic law works. If you get a conservative government which comes in and does exactly the things that previous conservative governments had done – which brought in fifty years of labor-party government – you will get back to the earlier pattern of events.

Now if central banks were together to take a somewhat more expansionary path – not deterred by the consideration that if they do something now they may overdo it – they may have to underdo it later. To me that's a virtue. When Paul Volcker in 1982 did what he did, all the monetarists in the world – that's a shrinking number, but it's not yet an empty set – said, 'Crime, crime, crime! He should not have done that'. Then, when Volcker saw that the recovery was a strong one, maybe even becoming over-strong, he did what every sailor does: he went on a different tack; he took in, with the result that the monetarists did not approve of him. They convicted him of a double crime. Professor Friedman predicted that in six months, there was going to be simultaneously an outburst of inflation and an outburst of unemployment. Now that's a new theory of stagflation, and it comes about because he had a two-year lag on the monetary mechanism, working completely independently of a shorter lag on the fiscal mechanism. If Christopher Johnson is worried that there may be trouble downstream from taking action now, I have to say that my kind of adviser will at that time be hanging generals, hanging central bankers, for not taking remedial action. Now you may overshoot, but I don't think that the evidence is in that any use of information and intelligence in a lean-against-the-wind, countercyclical fashion by both fiscal authorities and central banking authorities will be counterproductive, but that was what a minority of our profession was trying to sell the world for many years.

Solomon: I'm not going to defend central bankers at this point. We've just heard from Paul Samuelson, though only two of us around the table are former central bankers.

Cooper: You're forgetting Professor Solow, who was a part-time central banker.

Solomon: Three of us around the table.

Mundell: And Dick Cooper.

Solomon: And Dick also. And Randall Hinshaw! I'm sorry.

Cooper: So much for empirical generalizations.

Solomon: I'd better stick to theory; I was wrong on the facts. I put my two fingers up when Paul was talking about the fixed exchange-rate system in Europe. I agree with his main point that it was premature to go to that system and that some absurdities were perpetrated, the most spectacular one being the 500 percent briefly held discount rate in Sweden. But I thought the record should include a few words about policy in France. The Bank of France has taken every opportunity it could to lower interest rates, given the exchange-rate policy. To understand the French position on exchange-rate policy, one has to look back at French history. I think it's important to put that policy against the background of a country that had very high inflation over many years and an exchange rate that depreciated over a long period. The French are very proud of the fact that they have finally achieved a stable exchange rate and an inflation rate lower than Germany's, and it happens to be important to them. We can disagree with their value judgment, but I think we at least ought to understand how that value judgment was arrived at.

Samuelson: By the way, Léon Blum said exactly the same thing. In the late 1930s, after the whole sterling bloc had successfully benefited from depreciation, and after Belgium had successfully benefited from it, the French defended the gold parity in 1936, 1937, 1938, 1939, up to the time of the war itself.

Solomon: I have to say *touché*.

McCracken: I held up my hand several minutes ago, and in the interim several of the points that I wanted to make have been made. I don't think there's any question that monetary policy – primarily monetary policy – will have to be moving in a more expansionist direction. I was very much impressed with what Jim Tobin talked about a few minutes ago – that we've had other times of prolonged unemployment when there was considerable discussion that it was somehow inherent in the structure of things. I remember a conference out here in California in the early 1960s when Arthur Burns and I were among the people there. Arthur made a case that the unemployment problem was primarily structural. Once again, when we started to pursue appropriately expansionist policies, we found that the operating rate of the economy came up, and the unemployment rate settled back down to a reasonable level. One of the few advantages of old age is that you have a personal recollection of the growing span of history. In earlier periods of prolonged recession and unemployment, there was always grave concern as to whether this time economic policy would work. My guess is that, once again, expansionist economic policies will be successful.

Chancellor Kohl in a speech recently said that one of the major objectives this year is going to be to do something about unemployment. Now it may be that the election is the primary thing he had in mind, but I suspect not entirely. I would vote at this stage that we have to start moving, responsibly of course – we don't have to drive with the foot either all the way down on the accelerator or all the way down on the brake pedal – but to move deliberately and sensibly.

Having said this, if I may just add a footnote on structural unemployment. An interesting question for anyone who has spent his time in a school of business administration is what the structural employment implications may be of the flattening of the management structure. We're seeing a good deal of downsizing, and we hear a great deal about the elimination of layers of management. This clearly has implications for our highly educated management people coming out of our major universities.

Mundell: I want to follow up on some remarks that Paul Samuelson made. I too would give Paul Volcker high marks as a central banker – a B+ – but I think he started his disinflationary policy at least a year too late; he should have done it as soon as he was appointed. Now when we get to 1982, I wouldn't give him complete credit for the expansion. I think some credit has to go to the fiscal side. First of all, the stimulus effects, the supply-side effects, of the tax cuts raised the after-tax marginal efficiency of capital, and promoted the foundations of recovery. And in the second place, the fiscal expansion resulting from the acceleration of the military program had its own Keynesian effect. I think the fiscal expansion was the major thrust of the recovery, and I think you can prove that, because if it was primarily a monetary expansion that brought about the recovery, you'd have seen the expansion associated with a fall in real interest rates. But, in fact, it was the opposite; you had rising real interest rates, and that meant that the basic explanation for the recovery was the fiscal thrust in 1982.

Now we come to the question of central bank independence. We should notice that from the very beginning, the earliest central banks were by and large independent. The Bank of England was a private company up until 1945, and there was almost no interference with central banks during the period of the gold standard, when being a central banker wasn't all that powerful, because the commitment to maintain the gold parity meant that monetary policy had to be geared to the balance of payments. So there wasn't very much independent monetary policy. If you have a fixed exchange-rate system, and it's a real fixed exchange-rate system, with no possibility of devaluation, I would have no problem whatsoever with central bank independence. We don't live in that world today, so I do have a problem, and I think I agree with Paul's remark about Governor Crow.

The central bank is not independent in Canada, but is under the thumb of the Minister of Finance. However, John Crow was much smarter, if I may say so, than any of the Ministers of Finance that were in power. Michael Wilson, a bond salesman, knew nothing about monetary policy, and he allowed Governor Crow to have his way when Crow announced a monetary policy aimed at zero inflation in Canada. Now the Canadian economy is dominated by the US economy, and it's very hard to get it to diverge from what's happening in the United States. When the Crow policy started in 1987, the United States had an inflation rate of 4 percent, so in order to get zero inflation in Canada, interest rates after adjustments would have to be 4 percentage points below US rates, and with the same growth of productivity in the two countries, which is about right, wage-rate growth in Canada would have to be 4 percentage points lower than US wage-rate growth. There was absolutely no way in which anyone could do a public relations job even if the Bank of Canada had understood the needs in this transition. So what happened was a period of 15 percent interest rates in Canada when US interest rates were $7^1/2$ or 8 percent. This created a great influx of capital into Canada, leading to an appreciation of the Canadian dollar, which went from 69 cents in 1985 to 90 cents under Crow. The result was mass unemployment – this for a country that for forty years had tracked the US economy. If you look at the US unemployment rate, you find something close to the Canadian unemployment rate unless there has a been a big change in policy, as there was in this case. As I and others predicted, the Crow policy collapsed, and the Canadian dollar came back down, but the policy had killed off a whole sector of export industries.

So I think if you have an independent central bank that is not constrained by a fixed exchange rate, you make the central banker far too powerful a person unless you are going to make this an elected office. I agree that if exchange rates are flexible, the central bank should be under the thumb of the government. Of course, even in those countries that do have a kind of independent central bank, the exchange rate is always under the control of the Minister of Finance. Because of that, even if the central bank is ostensibly independent, the government could always force it to operate the way the government wanted by assigning a particular exchange-rate policy. Germany is the one case that has its own law, but even in Germany I think you'll find that the senior official at the IMF is never the head of the Bundesbank; it's the Minister of Finance. And that's true for the United States; the Secretary of the Treasury is the senior official at the IMF meetings.

My last comment is on the unemployment problem in Europe. I think we need to divide the unemployment into its different components. Some percentage undoubtedly is of the Keynesian kind that can be reduced by changing the exchange rate or by some kind of expansionary policies. But we can't ignore the other kinds of unemployment, and it is not enough to call all long-term unemployment structural. I would call attention to the unemployment that results from social programs that encourage people not to work. I suspect – I haven't looked into this carefully – that you'll find the mass unemployment in Spain is associated with a change in social programs around 1977–79 under the new government. I think what happened was that suddenly a whole new class of people – largely, quite often, women who had never been in the labor force or had any experience as employees – would register and then get on the unemployment rolls. Tom Willett asked for topics for graduate students. I think a good graduate student could do a wonderful and important thesis by looking at unemployment in cases like southern Italy and Spain to try to see how much of it is actual unemployment and how much is due to the social programs. This doesn't necessarily mean that you want to change the social programs; you may want to keep them, but in that case you don't have to treat this as a problem.

Tobin: On the question of who controls the exchange rate in the United States, it's officially the Treasury, but the only really strong instrument for doing anything about the exchange rate is the interest rate, and the Federal Reserve controls interest rates. I don't know of any situation in which the Treasury has said to the Federal Reserve that it could not move the interest rate the way it would like to for domestic policy reasons because that would move the exchange rate in a direction the Treasury wouldn't like. I think the Treasury's sovereignty over the exchange rate in the United States is mythical.

Cooper: Let me just underline Bob Mundell's last observation on researchable topics. I won't go into my anecdotes on Spain, but they strongly reinforce what Bob has said. It involves a type of research, I suspect, which graduate students in economics don't do very much these days – namely, go out into the field and actually talk to people. Some of this stuff is not the kind of thing you can get just by looking at IMF data tapes.

Solow: I would like to say a word about some serious research – not anecdotes – which has been done in the United States that goes very much against the idea that people would prefer to receive unemployment benefits rather than work. Unfortunately, this research is confined to the US, and says nothing about what might be true elsewhere. But the research rejects the notion that ordinary people – not like us – don't want to work, and prefer to sponge off unemployment insurance or the welfare system. I've worked for many years with a nonprofit corporation in New York that is in the business of conducting well-designed statistical experiments on things like this, with random assignments and control groups. The whole thing is done as much like agricultural research as can possibly be arranged. We have analyzed data from more than a dozen state-run experiments in the US on what is usually called 'workfare' – arrangements whereby people are required to work for their welfare or unemployment-insurance benefits. And then there have been very careful interview studies of participants in these programs, most of whom, by the way, are women with small children.

What has been found universally is that, first of all, participation in programs of this sort have small, but statistically significant positive effects on the longer-term earning capacity and employability of the people who are involved. Moreover, by an unmistakably large margin, the subjects in experiments like this, most of whom are women as I said, prefer the job to the transfer payment. In fact, most of them behave exactly like ordinary Americans. After three or four months, they are convinced that they're worth far more than they're being paid, but with very few exceptions they say, 'I would much rather have this job and be paid this piddling amount than have the same amount of money as a transfer payment'. Now these are Americans, and they are infected, no doubt, by American mores and what passes for proper belief in the US, but the experience of looking at the data, I have to say, leaves me skeptical of arguments that suggest that there is a lot of exploitation of the transfer mechanism. I think the transfer mechanism will be exploited as long as job opportunities are not available. None of these women say, 'I would rather have no transfer payment and no job rather than a transfer payment and no job'. What they say is, 'I would prefer a job and the payment rather than idleness'.

McKenzie: I think the important thing to remember is that unemployment does usually involve some decision. And many people who are unemployed – they may not be drawing unemployment benefits – may be living with their family or living off of accumulated assets. They don't accept a job unless the job is an improvement in their situation and does not prejudice their future as they see it.

Solow: Quite right.

McKenzie: So when graduate students are doing their studies of this problem, they should analyze the decision-making process and everything that affects it.

Solow: I quite agree. I should add that I made no suggestion that anyone would like to work for half of what is available as a transfer payment. No one – well, hardly anyone – would be that noble.

Mundell: I can understand that this test measures what people really believe. I think that people, by and large, would much prefer to have a solid job and have the self-esteem that goes with the fact that they're working rather than being paid without working. The study Bob Solow referred to looked only at the United States, where unemployment is more short term than in Europe. There's a lot more emphasis on long-term unemployment in Europe, and that's what we think of as noncyclical unemployment – the type that is not susceptible to ordinary macroeconomic policy.

Cooper: We are privileged to have in the audience Professor Ansley Coale, the noted demographer, who would like to make a comment.

Ansley J. Coale: I just wanted to mention something that's way back in history, but pertinent to the question about the way unemployed people behave. My mentor, Frank Notestein, who opened the Office of Population Research in the mid-1930s and did a lot of early pioneering research for which he is very well known, did a piece of research on a controversy in the thirties as to whether people on relief were encouraged to have babies – which would be a bad thing. What Notestein did was to get a matched sample of women who were on relief and women who weren't on relief, and he allowed for their education, duration of marriage, and so on; and the difference with respect to having babies was nil. If you allowed for the level of education, the background of employment, and so on, it didn't matter whether the women were on relief or not. I think it's interesting that there was already a controversy about this in the 1930s and that the particular comparison I mentioned turned out not to make a difference.

Cooper: If I could just comment, I'm delighted to hear that Bob Solow is involved in this organization that does serious social scientific research. President Clinton in his State of the Union message referred to this kind of situation the other day, and gave what he interpreted to be the decisive reason for a preference which these studies show – namely, that when kids ask other kids in school what their mother did, they could say that she does such and such rather than that she's on welfare.

Paul Samuelson has reminded us that we should not make policy on the basis of anecdotes, and he's quite right on that, but the anecdote I want to give is on the other side of what Bob Solow said, although not in contradiction, because it involves different things. In Spain, I'm told, there's a substantial putting-out system, early nineteenth-century style, in Barcelona and Catalonia whereby firms engage people to work in their homes – anything that can be done in the home: apparel industry, electronic industry, and so forth. A lot of immigrants from other parts of Spain, particularly from the poorer areas, come into Catalonia, go on to the unemployment rolls – not the welfare rolls but the unemployment rolls – and they work at home at the same time. Spain's registered unemployment is 22 percent, and a good research topic, it seems to me, is to take this observation that I've made and quantify it. Is it just an anecdote or is it quantitatively important?

Solow: There's undoubtedly some of that going on.

Cooper: And that involves field research. I think the injunction to be made is that on a priori grounds one would expect some cheating in the system. How much is there? That's some of the research that needs to be done.

5. Policy Implications of the Downturn in Japan

Introduced by Mikio Wakatsuki

Chairman Cooper: Although we have not resolved all of Europe's problems, I propose that we leave Europe, at least temporarily, and turn first to Japan, which is a country that has hardly been mentioned this morning but is extremely important in terms of the overall character of the world economy, and then turn to US macroeconomic policy, which we have touched on glancingly this morning. I'd like to ask Mr Wakatsuki, who has come all the way from Tokyo to be at this conference, to lead off the discussion on Japan.

Mikio Wakatsuki: First of all, I'd like to say that I'm very pleased and honored to be able to participate in this very prestigious conference. As some of you may know, according to the Chinese calendar, 1994 is the Year of the Dog, but in Japan some people are calling it the Year of the Puppy, because the economy is shrinking. Well, whether it's a puppy or not, the Japanese economy is really very dormant, just like a lazy dog. We are now having perhaps the longest, hardest and most serious recession in the post-World War II period. According to the official chronology, the current slump started in May 1991, which means that we are already in a state of slump for almost three years. The longest Japanese recession, which lasted three years, was after the first oil crisis. In terms of the depth of the decline, the worst one was in 1974, and it's quite likely that we may have negative growth for fiscal 1993.

So what went wrong? Basically, it's a cyclical phenomenon. That means we did too much in the late 1980s and we are now paying the bill. One could say, 'The higher the mountain, the deeper the valley'. What made the ups and downs even sharper was the overconfidence – or you might call it arrogance. In the late 1980s, people behaved as if the expansion would last forever. This kind of overconfidence still prevailed even after the implosion of the bubble. People thought we could make a sort of soft landing – adjustment without pain, because the Japanese economy was different and resilient, we thought. And this was of course wrong. Whatever adjustment is needed has to be done; otherwise, the next stage of expansion will not start.

So this is what we are now tackling. We are now having three types of adjustment. One is the so-called stock adjustment in productive capacity and in consumer durable goods – big-ticket items. In the latter half of the 1980s up until 1990, we invested very heavily because the financing costs were so low. At one time, in fiscal 1990, fixed investment comprised 20 percent of our GNP, and the stock of capital capacity increased by close to 9 percent. After the implosion of the bubble, we are having a decline in fixed investment. The stock adjustment in consumer durables is perhaps in its final stage. Sales of passenger automobiles have been declining for the past three years, and perhaps because of changes in spending patterns and the uncertainty ahead, people are still not resuming the purchase of those big-ticket items.

A second adjustment is the so-called Bond Street adjustment. The hardest hit, of course, are the financial institutions, construction companies and the real-estate business. The most serious group are the financial institutions, and the bad-loan problems will be here for some time. The third type of adjustment is restructuring. Because of the bubble days, many businesses overexpanded. Overemployment is a serious problem, but as recently as, say, two years ago, Japanese business's major concern was the labor shortage. Businesses tried hard to attract labor in view of the rapidly aging society. But now many companies are having the problem of excess workers. During the bubble days, they perhaps tried to have too frequent model changes, too many product arrays, and perhaps overproduction, so now they are really trying to rationalize their product lines and revise their investment pattern of model changes.

Employment adjustment in Japan is a serious matter. Companies are facing a very hard choice of either laying off workers or prolonging the adjustment period. Thus far, companies are doing all sorts of labor adjustment short of laying off workers: the cutting of overtime, the elimination of temporary workers, work-shift changes and the suspension of recruiting. As yet, we are not seeing any massive layoff. One reason is that companies are still having some resources because of the past bumper years, but if this slump is protracted, they face serious decisions. According to a recent survey, opinion is divided whether to maintain life-long employment or not; 47 percent say a certain revision is necessary, and another 47 percent say, well, we have to stick with this. So now opinion is equally divided. But most of the executives I've talked to still think the total cost of maintaining life-long employment is much lower than the cost of abandoning the policy if you include its social cost: social unrest, lowered labor morale, unemployment payments, and so on. But I don't know how long we can stick to this. These three types of adjustment all take quite some time – a year or two years or even longer. Some of these problems are very familiar to the United States. I remember, maybe a couple of years ago, Alan Greenspan saying that the US economy was facing a 50-mile-an-hour headwind, and he advocated balance-sheet adjustment and restructuring. We are perhaps following the same pattern as the United States did at that time.

We are also having another very difficult adjustment – namely, political adjustment. Of course the political adjustment has quite a lot to do with economics, and at this moment we are not sure whether the present prime minister will survive or not. But one thing is quite clear: his eight-party coalition cannot be stable. It will take at least another general election for the Japanese economy to become a little more stable and for the political picture to become clear.

So what should we do? All the economists except some government officials say that we need the Keynesian type of demand expansion, mostly by fiscal means, and there is a virtual consensus that we are going to have another fiscal package that would include a big increase in government expenditures plus an undetermined amount of tax cuts. Also proposed are measures to deal with the bad-loan problem and to expedite write-offs. A similar problem is the so-called credit crunch, though it's not really a credit crunch, but banks are much less aggressive in extending credit than during the bubble period. So the measures to deal with the bad-loan problem are very important. On another matter, I don't like to use the very unpopular word 'structural', but structural policies are needed. What I mean by structural reform is deregulation. This is a catchword everywhere, but we really need deregulation in order to encourage business to get into a new business frontier like the advanced information and communication systems, like the US information superhighway, and so on. We also need to open up our market to more imports in order to narrow the price differentials between imports and domestic products. That would mean more consumption in real terms. And perhaps we should encourage more foreign direct investment. This would provide more competition, and would also stimulate demand. Another potential source of increased demand is our very quiet, peaceful tourist industry, which we are strongly encouraging. If these various measures are properly and effectively taken, we might be able to get back to the sustainable growth of 3 percent in 1995, though perhaps such a full-scale recovery can come back only after 1996.

This doesn't mean that I'm pessimistic about the medium-term outlook. The three elements which supported the past very strong growth of the Japanese economy are left intact: the very high savings rate, the very disciplined labor and the high-level technology, with a very high degree of productivity. What is lacking at this moment, perhaps, is aggressive entrepreneurship. Businesses are now a bit despondent because of the new elements in our cycle: the asset-price deflation which is very unfamiliar to the post-World War II Japanese economy and the loss of almost blind faith in the ever-rising value of land. So the way of doing business now must be revised. The investment pattern based on this kind of ever-rising prices has to be changed. With more deregulation and with a more open economy, we would have a more consumer-oriented society. And with this kind of emphasis, we can expect some revival in business confidence. One good thing is that Japan is surrounded by all these strong-growth Asian countries. I hope that business confidence is restored and that business takes advantage of the opportunities that are being opened by the new government program, which stresses deregulation and a more consumer-oriented Japanese economy.

Cooper: Thank you very much. I hope that in the discussion you will come back to two issues. One is to give us your judgment about the actual prospects of passage of the fiscal and deregulation measures – the timing and so forth – and the other is to say something about Japanese attitudes and policies toward the exchange rate and the external accounts. But Paul Samuelson would like to come in.

Samuelson: Well, Robert Frost said he had a lover's quarrel with the universe; I have a lover's quarrel with Japan. And with friends like me, Japan has no need for an enemy. I am the Long-Term Credit Bank of Japan Visiting Professor of Political Economy at NYU – it's the longest title in Christendom – and I have been nagging the Japanese for more than thirty years. I have to declare that Japan wins the prize for the best mismanaged economy in the world. It is a Keystone Kops scenario from beginning to end. At one end we have the Ministry of Finance, which consists of autonomous mandarins. Now this is completely different from, say, the excellent British civil service. My friend, Sir Frank Lee, could say to me, 'I am the man who nationalized steel'. But then he would say, 'Of course I didn't nationalize steel; I carried out my minister's orders. In the same way, I am the man who denationalized steel'.

Well, the mandarins in the Ministry of Finance, who are pretty good takers of examinations at Tokyo University School of Law – they're not very good lawyers – learn economics on the job, and they don't learn it very well. They really think they run things. And they're right to think that, because who is going to tell them nay? There has been a new man at the Bank of Japan. He has been a new man for so long that he's about to be rotated out of the job. He inherited what is admittedly a difficult problem – a bubble in being where land prices were rising exponentially. My colleagues at MIT argue whether it was a rational bubble or an irrational bubble. I don't care; it was a double bubble, and that is never an easy macroeconomic problem to prescribe for. We went through the same thing in America. I think I'm older than you are, Paul McCracken, and I can remember in my knickerbockers the economic controversy when Carl Snyder at the Federal Reserve Bank of New York and Professor Bullock at Harvard argued that we had to have a tight monetary policy forever because the stock market up until 1928 and 1929 went through either a rational or irrational bubble.

Tobin: You read about that later; you don't remember it from your knickerbocker days.

Samuelson: By the way, Jim, I have never contradicted you in my life [loud laughter]. Against Snyder and Bullock were Hawtrey and Keynes, whose advice was to think about the GNP and be eclectic. Well, the man from the Bank of Japan started out okay. The bubble didn't burst until the beginning of 1990. Once it burst, you got a rational or irrational negative bubble – antimatter – on the downside. Equity prices are something below 50 percent of their peak level, and land prices are somewhat down. The Bank of Japan again and again repeated the same error that our Federal Reserve did – too little and too late. Now if you look at a 2 percent interest rate, you may think, oh, well, they can't have done such a bad job. But you have to look at what the price-level behavior has been and at what is required in a long and sustained and serious recession – at what real interest rates are the optimum ones.

Why don't we get guidance from the Diet, from the legislature? Well, the Diet for thirty years was a faction-ridden, corruption-ridden group who could provide no continuity of leadership and certainly no rational intellectual leadership to a civil service. That system finally broke down; you got a popular prime minister who seems to retain his popularity while he does nothing. By the way, he no longer has the cards to do very much. There are only two things that society can depend upon: an opposition political party and a professional cadre of scientific economists who can give good advice. Well, Japan is the unluckiest country in the world. There's no opposition party that anyone would trust in the leftist parties of the last fifty years in Japan. And there is no cadre of regular academic and non-academic economists who are well trained in the problems that this kind of conference discusses. If you want to know about fixed-point theorems, there are plenty of very good Japanese economists. If you want to know nonsense about the transformation problem in Marx, there is a limited quantum of Marxist economists who still constitute at Tokyo University about 50 percent; you get an appointment, we get an appointment.

So the situation is a ship without control. Well now, let an outsider analyze what's wrong and what could be done. I give a lot of advice, and it's worth every dollar I'm paid for it. I write for *El País*, I write for *ABC*. In Madrid, I write for *Corriere*, and I have to admit that a small country in Europe has certain limitations on it through the exchange-rate and so forth. In the case of Japan, we've had a system which by great good luck and perhaps wisdom has been able to run a fiscal budget of great austerity for a decade. It has accumulated as a result a low public debt relative to GNP and a low – and probably negative – deficit, properly measured, as a fraction of GNP. These are the two measures that should be used always at the beginning. Japan has plentiful reserves. So here is a case where you cannot pity a country if it will not use that which it has. It has the elbowroom, and I think the implication is clear. I praised Paul Volcker because in 1982 he turned up the monetary tap successfully. I was reminded, half properly, by two people that I hadn't gone into Lafferism as the fiscal thing. Well, in the case of Japan, my doctrine is very simple. Chocolate is good, herring is good. We should have both in Japan: fiscal stimulus and whatever monetary stimulus is prudent in a recession situation. I'm always asked, how low should the interest rate be? I deplore anecdotes, but I use them all the time; Abraham Lincoln was asked how long should a man's legs be, and he replied, 'Long enough to reach the ground'. And that's how low the real interest rate ought to be in Japan for a measured period until the system responds.

The Japanese situation in my guess is worse than we think it is, because the Japanese are the best people in the world in covering up difficulties. The banking system in the US was in terrible shape not long ago because of the cover-up; the banking system in Japan is potentially in even worse shape. Now that's the prime candidate for a period of easier money. You remember how it was said just a few years ago that easier money wouldn't help here because it would be like pushing on a string? Think of where our banking system would be – and it's landing now – if we had not had as a result of nagging by your humble servant and important people on the Federal Reserve a very favorable carry of long-term securities, where the banks made a juicy profit and paid a very small amount in investment. They're now in a position where they're actually interested in making some old-fashioned loans. The Japanese banking system is going to have to get a massive infusion, comparable to what the FDIC and the FSLIC have done for our banking system. That's just writing off old losses. It will add to the public debt relative to the GDP of Japan but, unlike Belgium and Italy, Japan has a very comfortable margin for that.

Finally, the lifetime employment system is a lousy system. It's a comfortable system for each personality, but if Japan needs to re-orient itself with respect to domestic sectors versus traditional export sectors, it is inhibited in that it has to work with an immobilized group, as happens under lifetime employment. Well, I'm sure the lifetime employment system is going to erode under present conditions, and I could be very confident and optimistic about the Japanese, including their future rates of inflation, if I thought there was any likelihood of any action. However, we meet again and again in Washington and in the G–7; the Japanese listen and they say, 'Ah, so, ah, so', and we stupidly think that means they agree and are going to go home and act. What they mean is, 'We hear you, we're going to listen, we're going to think about it'.

I don't know what the next step has to be with respect to political reform, but I do know this: that macroeconomic alleviation should not have to wait on solving every corruption problem in Japan and that deregulation, which in general every sophomore in economics is in favor of, is not going to do anything about the business-cycle situation. It is scandalous that the Ministry of Finance comes in and says, 'Well, okay, we'll give you some fiscal expansion; we'll talk about an income-tax cut, but of course we have to couple it with an increase in the value-added tax'. What is needed is not preserving the reputation of the Ministry of Finance in creating austerity for the public sector of Japan; what's needed is a net stimulus from the fiscal side. They don't know and I don't know and our representative from Japan doesn't know whether thirty months is the right lag after which Japan will be on its way to overheating its economy and it will be proper to put in a value-added tax at that time to offset an income-tax reduction. Trying to do day-by-day policy on the basis of a correct diagnosis of events four years ahead is a very stupid way of running the ship.

So I guess this boils down to something that sounds terrible: why doesn't Europe, why doesn't Japan look to the marvelous USA and do the things which we have been doing so successfully? I don't speak as an American patriot; there's no government I like to criticize more than our own, but when we're in recession we have been doing something. We have been on the mildly aggressive Keynesian tack twice: in the earlier 1980s and now. It has worked well for us; we have been a very good neighbor and servant to the world. Twice our locomotive has moved, giving the other locomotives a chance to move. Well, as Rex Harrison said, 'Why can't a woman be more like a man?'. Why can't Western Europe, particularly those countries with elbowroom – and Japan – be more like the good old USA?

Mundell: I wonder if, to some extent, the difference in views between the United States and Japan reflects different objective functions. When Japan looks at its policies and its opportunities compared with the United States, it really prefers the situation it's in to the situation of the Americans. I was looking the other day at the current-account balances of different countries, and from 1982 until 1993 the United States had a cumulative current-account deficit of $1.1 trillion. Over the same period, Japan had a cumulative current-account surplus of something like $800 billion (that includes 1993, when the current-account surplus amounted to $128 billion).

Now what this means is that Japan has been building up equity in the world economy at the rate of $100 billion a year, more or less, and has the largest net equity position that any country at any time in history has ever acquired. The United States, on the other hand, has built up a net debtor position, although we don't know exactly how to measure assets abroad. Looking back from the late 1970s, when the United States was by far the biggest net creditor in the world, it lost that position, not to Japan, but to Saudi Arabia for a couple of years around 1981, and then in 1986 the United States became a net debtor, with Japan replacing Saudi Arabia as having the largest creditor position. Some time in the future, Japan is going to have assets abroad of well over $1 trillion, and will be able to live on the income from that for decades even with no new investment and with a trade deficit of something like $100 billion a year. In view of the phasing of the Japanese aging structure compared to the American, this change in the Japanese current-account position will be a good thing.

Now I think that most of Paul Samuelson's criticisms of Japan are well taken, but they should be put in the perspective that Japan is still the best economy in the world from the standpoint of unemployment rates – far better than any of the European economies and better than the United States. And Japan has had a lower inflation rate over this period. Its big problem, of course, is that it's in a crisis now, but I think to a large extent that crisis is US-made. It comes about in part because of Japan-bashing and because the Secretary of the Treasury, Lloyd Bentsen, acting on advice of his MIT-trained Council of Economic Advisers, says, 'Appreciate the yen'. But Paul doesn't say that; he says, 'Increase the money supply', and of course if that's the right policy for Japan, the yen will come down. Then Lloyd Bentsen will be mad at Japan, and there will be another international incident. There's an issue here of playing a kind of power politics. If Japan moves in the way it should to restimulate its economy in the right way by monetary policy – and I agree that this is absolutely the right policy for Japan – the dollar will go up against the yen to something like 125, 130, 135, which is probably more or less where it belongs. But the US treasury isn't going to permit it; it will threaten to do A, B, C and D, and Japan, in its weak political position at this time, just can't take on the United States.

Samuelson: I would like to comment on one aspect of what you said: whether the Japanese have different goals from us and whether they are happy in the bed which they have made for themselves. Everything you said would have been perfectly correct, in my judgment, up to 1988. They liked the bubble in being, they liked the favorable trade surplus, they liked the acquiring of assets abroad, particularly since they were very gullible in what they thought was the value of those assets that were being sold to them. If you think that today the Japanese representative person is an extremely happy, serene, unworried person – who was the fellow who wrote about Martin Luther's identity crisis?

Solow: Erik Erikson.

Samuelson: If Luther were alive now, he could go to Japan and have great patience with the Japanese, because they're in an identity crisis. What happened to this marvelous management system they had which worked by consensus? What happened to their just-in-time inventory accumulation? Every Japanese business that I talked to says, 'US business is wonderful; in Japan our business is terrible'. It's so terrible that they're actually insourcing Honda building and so forth, not because it's cheaper; it's more expensive, but the true cost under a lifetime security system of using workers who are not unemployed but who are producing nothing that is useful in response to the market – that was Brezhnev's kind of productivity. He kept up the work; there was no unemployment. It's what Joan Robinson used to call 'disguised unemployment', and I think, Jim, I remember that from my own studies and not from reading about it in the history books. I think the Japanese people are very shaken.

Mundell: I think you're right again. I agree that the Japanese don't like the business position they're in now, and I think they don't like this in part because the appreciated yen has started to price them out of the market over a wide range of different things. It has cut into profits. It has now overpriced things in Japan, and I think it's the source of simply everything that's wrong in Japan: the depression, the stock market, the tight-money policy that is forced on Japan by the unfortunate attempt on the part of the United States to get the Japanese to appreciate the exchange rate – to about 35 percent above what it should be.

Solomon: I have to say, Bob, that what I've just heard is slightly absurd.

Mundell: What is slightly?

Solomon: Perhaps we can come back to that. May I make a diplomatic point here? I have the impression that when we Americans talk about the Japanese, we are much harsher in our criticism of them than we are of our friends in Europe and elsewhere. That's what I judge from what I read in the newspapers and, I'll be very frank to say, that's what I judge from what I've heard here in the last half hour. I don't know why it is. It's not right. Let's have a little more equality in our treatment of our friends around the world.

Cooper: I have a comment on what Bob Mundell said, since he alluded to the MIT-trained economists at the Treasury – and one might add the Yale-trained economists.

Tobin: He also referred to the economists at the Council of Economic Advisers.

Cooper: The Treasury and the Council. According to the people below the Secretary of the Treasury (I exclude the Secretary, about whom I have some doubts), the deal as I understand it was that if Japan were to do what Paul Samuelson wants it to do, they would find a return of the yen to 120 or 125 to the dollar quite acceptable. But the view was that in the absence of stimulative policy – and the focus was on the fiscal side – the yen should and must appreciate. Above all, the Treasury did not want the Japanese to intervene in the foreign-exchange market to keep the yen from appreciating. In other words, the deal was designed to present the Japanese with the alternative of either undertaking some fiscal stimulus or accepting the consequences of an appreciation of the currency. Now exclude the Secretary of the Treasury because, at least judging from his past behavior, it wouldn't surprise me if there were a component of genuine preference for appreciation of the yen that had to do with protecting competing American firms and industries against their Japanese competitors. But as far as the Yale- and MIT-trained economists are concerned, I'm quite sure that I've stated the correct propositions. So the way Bob Mundell put it is somewhat misleading.

Morris: Dick, I know you're right on what you said, because I've spent a lot of time talking to those underneath the Secretary of the Treasury. I must say that I very much agree with Bob Solomon's last comment on the dialogue concerning Japan. I think that we are overly harsh, strident and 'big stick' in our approach, and I would like to see that go, although I've been accused recently of being slightly critical of Japan. I think the timing of what we've been doing in US policy is very inappropriate – to use the big stick for trade-related purposes at a time when Japan is going through what I would regard as a fundamental social reform. I think Professor Samuelson was dead right when he talked about the looming of what could be a financial crisis in Japan. There's a very good study by a Harvard professor, who puts the non-performing loans of the twenty-one largest Japanese banks at 30 trillion yen. This, obviously, is going to be a big cost for Japan over time. Everyone agrees that Japan needs to take some kind of fiscal stimulus, and people could agree on many other things that Japan needs to do. However, within Japan there is not the kind of consensus, the social and political impetus, to do these things. This is something we don't seem to understand when we're looking at Japan with a big stick, saying do this, do that. Another factor we haven't talked much about today is the aging of Japan's population, which is more rapid than in most places, forcing the Japanese to look at what sort of a social safety net they need to adopt over time. This is something that is very often left out of the whole view of Japan's economy, and it needs to be addressed.

Johnson: I would like to put in a word in favor of the appreciation of the yen as the correct long-term policy for Japan. My main reason is that Japan, like Germany, has tended to linger rather too long in various manufacturing sectors, which countries such as the USA and the UK have got out of – not without a certain amount of transitional pain and bemoaning the past glories of the automobile industry and all that. But it is surely logical that Japan should make the same move that the US has made toward more of a service economy. This also involves moving more out of agriculture, which still takes a disproportionate part of Japan's manpower. And the way the mechanism can work is through currency appreciation and outsourcing of Japanese manufacturing industry through Japanese direct investment in the Tiger countries of Southeast Asia. We've seen this process going on, and I don't see any particular reason to try to arrest or reverse it. The Japanese all appear to have accepted this policy in the late 1980s when they had an economic boom. The appreciation of the yen was fine, and they were looking forward to the day when not only would they have a greater GNP per head than the United States but a greater total GNP than the United States, because the higher value of the yen would have raised the value of their gross national product so much. Well, I suppose the reason why they don't still believe that is that they have a recession, so we come back to the point that they do need to do more to reflate the economy by fiscal policy. This they can afford to do better than most other countries because the size of their deficit is much smaller than that of their trading partners. The more we can do to conquer their reservations about having a bigger budget deficit – and I know many of us have been trying – the better it will be for all of us.

Cooper: I'd like to make a couple of observations and then turn the floor back to Mr Wakatsuki for any final observations he wants to make, including comments on the questions that have been raised. We have seen unemployment rise in Japan from around 2 percent to 2.8 percent, where I think it is now – modest by the standards of other countries. But one of the practices in Japan, as I understand it – and Mr Wakatsuki alluded to it – is that when demand weakens, so-called temporary workers, who are not part of the permanent workforce, are let off. They do not join the unemployed; they withdraw from the labor force.

In response to Bob Solomon's remark about the different treatment of Japan, I think it is correct that American comment on

Japan is different in quality from the way it is on Europe, and it is for my taste much too trenchant. I don't want to defend the trenchancy of the comment, but I do want to defend some asymmetry in treatment between Japan and Europe. My observation – and it's not mine alone; it is shared, I know, by at least some Japanese – is that in a real sense in terms of policy the official opposition in Japan has been the US government. In Britain, the Tory government has the Labour Party in opposition; in Germany, the SPD is in opposition to the CDU; and so forth. There has not been in Japan an effective domestic opposition until possibly recently. We may now be in a watershed in that regard, but for the past thirty years there has not been an effective internal opposition in Japan. That function has been performed by the US government, and this means that the US government has gotten into the interstices of domestic policy issues in Japan in a way which would be regarded as offensive and which the US generally eschews as far as other countries are concerned. In Japan it has been resented by some, but accepted by much of the population, particularly – or maybe I should say only – when, in their hearts, the Japanese public knew the Americans were right. As long as we took positions which made sense, we had what you might call a silent majority of support in Japan for changes in policy.

Let me give two examples. One is rice policy, which is a very emotive issue in Japan. But there are a lot of Japanese consumers who say, in effect, 'Basically, the Americans are right. Why should we be paying five or six times the world price of rice?'. And while they're reluctant to come out domestically and say so, nonetheless they're silently cheering for a change in policy. Another issue concerns aviation. For years JAL, Japan Airlines, was the monopolist airline of Japan in international aviation, and the domestic airlines could not break into that. It was with American help, often allied with a domestic Japanese partner – sometimes silent, sometimes overt – that policy changes got made. This is a peculiar relationship which has been built since the 1950s; it may not survive, and it may not need to survive, with the rapid political transformation in Japan. But it has existed during this period, and it gives rise, I think naturally, to a somewhat different US treatment and, in particular, to getting more into domestic policies than would otherwise be done. To say that is not to support the trenchancy that one sometimes sees in American journalists and in political statements about Japan.

My final observation is about the aging of Japan. We've heard about this for a long time. The Japanese use it, I believe, as an excuse for doing nothing. It is true that the age profile of the Japanese population shows a rapid degree of aging. But we're all on the same trend; it's only the slope of the schedule which is at issue, and one could argue that the Japanese more rapid aging justifies a somewhat higher aggregate savings rate than would be true in other countries. But that is not adequate to justify the very hard fiscal policies that the Japanese have taken, come hell or high water, in the lasts ten years. Having said that, let us give Mr Wakatsuki the last word.

Wakatsuki: Well, thank you very much. I accept the various comments as friendly advice. Things are changing, and inevitably that takes time, partly because, as the chairman mentioned, we perhaps didn't have an effective opposition party. Our system, which was formed in 1955, functioned well until the late 1980s. Now people are realizing that more emphasis should be put on the consumer side; the consumer should get more benefit from economic growth. Our system, which lasted for more than four decades, has collapsed, but unfortunately a new one has not yet been formed, so we have to be patient.

On the exchange rate, I agree with Mr Johnson's comment that we need perhaps a little slant toward a stronger yen over a long period of time, although I think it's wrong for the United States to use this as a short-term weapon. There should be a more consistent trend toward a stronger yen – not such a rapid appreciation. I recall that after the Plaza and Louvre accords, US pressure was so strong that the yen appreciated from 240 to 120, and this rapid appreciation caused tremendous problems. Too rapid change in such a basic economic variable as the exchange rate creates confusion and dislocation, and that, I think, is not very good strategy. In the aftermath of the sharp appreciation of the yen and the tremendous deflationary impact on the Japanese economy, all the outcry was for a more stimulative package rather than for structural change because the deflationary impact was so acute. And as the stimulatory measures became effective, all talk about structural reform was forgotten. We thought we had changed the structure of the economy, but that was due to the boom. When the bubble burst, nothing – maybe – had changed.

About the lifelong employment system, it is certainly true that many people think that in the long run the system cannot continue. It is up to each industry whether to maintain the system or not. Some industries think the system will break down, and there are already signs. It's a social pressure mainly on management. If a company lays off workers, it is regarded as a disgrace for management and a breach of the understanding that what is good for the company is good for the worker. But many people – nearly half of the executives surveyed – are of the opinion that the lifelong employment system may need to be revised and perhaps cannot be continued. However, in view of our present troubles, now is probably not a good time to abandon the system.

On the bad-loan situation, it is true that this is a big problem. The problem may be exaggerated, but this is our own fault, because we don't have your disclosure system in the United States. At this time, there is strong criticism in Japan of using official money to bail out the problem banks. Some of the strong banks can manage without help. For the weak banks, this will take quite a long time. The first priority should be to make write-offs easier without too much intervention by the Ministry of Finance. There is also a need to develop a market where banks can sell the bad loans.

Turning to the developing countries, they now have a better quality and wider array of products that can be used in Japan. Of course some people are complaining. The competition from imports is getting fierce, but the trend of the day is toward a more consumer-oriented society, and when this current difficult recession period is over, we should have brisk two-way transactions. And I think that in the long run this will be beneficial both for the developing countries and for Japan.

6. Macroeconomic Policy Dilemmas in the United States

Introduced by James Tobin

Chairman Cooper: We now leave the macroeconomic problems of Europe and Japan, and turn to those of the United States. Professor Tobin has agreed to introduce the discussion.

Tobin: A year ago, the new administration was faced with two problems in macroeconomics. One was the dissatisfaction of the country with the long-run potential growth of the economy. The capacity of the economy was not big enough, and wasn't growing fast enough. The productivity of labor had been stagnant or growing very slowly from approximately 1973 on, and real wages had not even been keeping up with productivity. So one problem the administration resolved to face was accelerating productivity over the long run. The second problem was that we were as a country not using fully the capacity that existed. This was a business-cycle problem – more of a short-run, we hope a short-run, difficulty. The trouble was that the two problems were not easily treatable by a single policy, since the long-run problem required more saving, the short-run problem possibly less saving. The long-run problem might be helped by reducing the budget deficit; the short-run problem might be helped by speeding up the recovery with at least temporary fiscal stimulus through tax cuts or additional expenditures.

At that point, the country had been for almost four years in what we might call a growth recession. According to the official National Bureau dating of recessions, we had a very short recession, limited to about two quarters in 1991, because the par for the National Bureau is zero, so only negative growth counts as recession. But if we take as par the sustainable growth rate at capacity operation for the US economy, which is around 2.2 to 2.5 percent per year, we would find that beginning with the second quarter of 1989, the economy fell short of that for three and a half years. Only in the fourth quarter of 1992 did the economy begin to exceed that, and it was not continued actually in the first part of 1993. So on these terms we had a long recession, in which we fell short of the potential growth of the economy for a long time – almost the whole of the Bush administration.

The recession was accompanied by a rise in unemployment. It was a shallow growth recession, because unemployment never rose to the levels it had risen in previous deep recessions, such as the one at the beginning of the 1980s. The peak unemployment rate was around 7.5 percent. But the so-called recovery was very disappointing, because it was going so slowly. Unemployment was not declining very much and was actually sometimes rising, so there was a lot of talk about a jobless recovery. My attitude toward that is that a jobless recovery is not a recovery. It just means that the growth of output is not sufficient, is not fast enough, to reduce unemployment or to reduce it at the speed accomplished in past recovery periods.

So the administration initially was thinking about having a temporary fiscal stimulus for the short-run problem – the cyclical recovery problem – and a budget package which would reduce the deficit over the longer term. That turned out not to be politically possible, or perhaps intellectually possible: to explain why one should do two things that seemed to be opposite. As you know, the administration first cut its aspirations for a fiscal stimulus to rather minor proportions, and then abandoned it altogether after a Republican filibuster in Congress. It was forced to accept a budget package which finally was passed by one vote.

That was an austerity budget really for the next five years. The administration then began to accept the view – it had no choice but to accept the view – that the fiscal restriction package was sufficient stimulus in itself because it would reduce long-term interest rates. This was an economic point argued by Martin Feldstein initially: that if you got the public to believe that there was going to be a reduced budget deficit in the future, then that would so reduce long-term interest rates that it would stimulate the economy in the present. And since something like this seemed to happen during the year, the administration is claiming credit both for the recovery and for the reduction in the budget deficit. My own opinion is that it was correct to think that we would have done better to have some fiscal stimulus at the beginning of the year; we'd be better off now if that had been done. But this president may share with Ronald Reagan one of the most necessary characteristics of a successful presidency – he's been lucky!

As for monetary policy, there was good reason to ask the Fed to lower interest rates further a year ago. The Feds held them constant, although it was tempted at various points to raise the short-term interest rates from 3 percent to a higher rate. It didn't do that, and maybe if the Fed continues to resist the pressure to raise rates just because recovery is proceeding, that in itself will be a different kind of policy than we usually have had in recoveries, and it may help to keep things going. Certainly the stock market has responded very favorably toward this policy.

Now the question is whether we are also making some progress on the long-run problem. In the ardor for fiscal austerity that we had last summer, the president was forced to abandon a number of public investment outlays that he had made a point of advocating strongly earlier. His idea was the logical one of figuring that if we were to have additional spending for infrastructure, education and other things of benefit for future generations, then this would perhaps be as good as deficit reduction itself – or better because of improving the productivity growth of the economy in the long run. But Congress made him give up a good part of those ambitions for having a public investment program. Originally, the idea could have been that we allow ourselves more deficit spending, but only for public investment projects that would be good for both the short-run and the long-run problems. We did have some evidence of improvements in productivity, but the jury is still out on whether these are cyclical – the normal more intensive use of labor that has been kept on the payrolls (not as extensively as in Japan, but practised in American companies too) – or whether there has been a permanent improvement either in the level of US productivity or in its rate of growth, or both. I'm inclined to believe that there has been some improvement permanently, because in this particular long and shallow recession, employers have had plenty of time to let their labor forces decline by attrition. Perhaps they entered the recovery period this year with less redundant labor still on the payrolls than would be normal in previous business cycles. But all this remains to be seen. We still have 6.4 percent unemployment – something like that. It's about a point above what I guess most people guess to be the lowest inflation-safe unemployment rate.

Samuelson: Are you saying that 5.4 percent is what most people consider to be the safe level of unemployment? By a point do you mean 100 basis points?

Tobin: I mean 1 percentage point – 100 basis points – to go from where we are to inflation-safe full employment, which is equivalent to something like 2.5 percent of real GDP. Now one question is, how much of a growth in actual GDP does it take to do that? It takes at least the sustainable rate of growth and then the additional amount needed to catch up, and that additional amount depends on how fast you want to get there. The administration is talking about getting to 5.5 or 5.4 percent unemployment in 1998, but getting pretty close to that even in 1996.

I must say I think the labor-market situation is worse in the United States than the unemployment rate suggests. There are several evidences of that. One was mentioned this morning, which is the surprisingly low amount of apparent vacancies in this economy, given where we are in unemployment. There are other statistics with the same message, such as the unusual prevalence of people who have lost their jobs as opposed to people who have voluntarily left their jobs. And we know we have this epidemic of downsizing going on. We have also the displacement of workers from the military and from the defense program in general.

Finally, I have to say that I find the following question something of a puzzle. The United States is a low-saving economy. In fact, that's the main criticism that we've made of our own economy for a long time. The criticism applies particularly, of course, when we're operating at full capacity. Then we don't save enough as a nation, and in consequence we have the macroeconomic reasons for having a big current-account deficit and for having a low rate of investment, especially investment that results in capital facilities we own – that we haven't mortgaged to lenders from abroad. And yet it seems to be very difficult to generate enough investment to absorb the small amount of saving of which this economy is capable at full employment. Why is that? I don't know; I don't know why we don't find it easier to absorb by investment outlays the small amount of saving that we are capable of doing when we're operating at capacity. One possibility that occurs to me is that we're having a lot of capital-augmenting technical progress going on, and so it doesn't take as much investment to raise productivity as we might have thought it would in the past.

As for the budget deficit, the administration's $500 billion in five years, roughly, actually will succeed in reducing the deficit to a point that's sustainable in the sense that it keeps the debt-to-GDP ratio from rising. We were in danger in the past of having such a large deficit in the budget that, given the interest charges on it, the ratio of debt to GDP would continually rise. We are now going to have the deficit low enough so that's not true when the five years are over in 1997. Whether this outcome will continue over the longer run will depend on arresting the projected rise in medical expenses by the government.

So maybe President Clinton will be lucky for another year, and we will continue to have this recovery.

Corden: May I start off by asking a question, maybe a naive question? President Bush lost the election apparently because of the state of the economy. The public is what you might call short-term Keynesian in its belief that the instruments of policy are available. President Clinton is getting the credit apparently for the improving state of the economy. Yet, when it comes to fiscal policy, the administration is not a free agent; it has to get the agreement of Congress. Any action takes time even if Congress can be made to agree. Monetary policy is under the control of the Fed, not the administration. It's rather curious, isn't it, that we associate the state of the economy with the administration when it really has so little power over it – particularly with respect to short-term policy. Of course it can do things for the long term; that's another question.

Tobin: Well, that's right, but in spite of that the president is going to be held responsible both for what the Congress does or doesn't do and for what the Fed does or doesn't do. He's going to hold the bag – that's for sure. But I think the public didn't believe that President Bush was concerned about the matter.

Corden: What could he have done?

Tobin: Well, he could have had a program that he asked the Congress to authorize other than lowering capital-gains taxes, which, for good reasons, didn't excite people as a remedy for the problems they were having in their own situations. I think the people in the Bush administration saw that the recession was shallow and not like the recession of 1980–82 or the previous one after the first oil shock, so they couldn't see why the American people were much more alarmed than they had seemed to be in those earlier occasions when the business cycle was much worse. They couldn't believe that they needed to do anything about it. They acted as if it was unreasonable that the public should be alarmed and worried. My interpretation is that the public detected that the administration didn't really think there was a problem.

McCracken: In partial answer to Max Corden's question, presidents of course take credit when things are rising, and the economy spends more time rising than declining. So the message gets through. On another matter, it is conceivable that in the couple of years ahead, we could be pleasantly surprised about the rate of growth in productivity. One of the somewhat overlooked aspects of the developments in the last year is the very strong pace of capital outlays, particularly in machinery and equipment – producers' durables. New orders for equipment are very strong, and if we get that kind of thing moving here, we might surprise ourselves with the resulting gains in productivity.

Randall Hinshaw: So far, we've been talking about the United States as a whole, but I want to remind us all, particularly those from the east coast, that we're presently in California, where the situation is much more serious than in the rest of the country. With a much higher unemployment rate than the US average, California is still very much in a recession, from which it doesn't appear to have recovered at all.

Tobin: Well, it's one-seventh of the national economy, so it's a big thing, for sure.

Cooper: California in the early 1980s had a boom which the rest of the country didn't have, partly because of the heavy concentration of defense spending here. The present situation is the other side of that – heavy dependence on one sector which has higher variation than many other sectors, at least in this period.

Tobin: The identification of which regions are in great trouble and which are booming has moved around a lot in recent years. The midwest, which was smoke-stack built, was down and is now doing very well. The southwest oil boom gave way to bad times there, while California was booming, and now it's the other way around.

Solow: Massachusetts experienced much the same thing as California and for the same reasons, but with a slightly different industrial composition. The difference is that the Massachusetts economy seems to have turned upward a little before California.

Cooper: It went down a little before California.

Solow: It went down a little before as well. It's also true, I think, that the people in the Clinton administration are thinking all the time about things they could do to help California that would have no budgetary impact whatsoever [laughter].

Mundell: Well, we've been talking about the last election and why Bush lost. What about the next election? If we take Jim Tobin's figures on the economy, but use the National Bureau guidelines, we're into about the tenth quarter of expansion–something like that. And if you go all the way through 1994 and 1995 in expansion, by the time you get up to something like the eighteenth quarter of expansion, isn't it really quite likely that 1996 is going to be a recession year? To avoid that, there will be a need to stimulate the economy, and I would just guess, looking ahead, since we do live in a world where savvy administration politicians know that they need an expanding economy in an election year, the best and possibly most likely way to keep the economy rolling past the election would be through some kind of prior tax cut. Now that may be a little bit overly cynical, but I wonder if the administration's goals aren't set too low. Given what Professor Solow has stated about the type of unemployment in the United States as being mainly of the Keynesian variety, then why should we be happy or satisfied with an unemployment rate of 5.5 percent? Why not go down to at least, let's say, the old Okun floor of 4 percent and shoot toward policies that will generate the expansion of the economy in that sense? If we believe the old Okun Law, then the economy is running now about $500 billion below capacity.

Solow: If I could just respond briefly to that, I don't think that there is anyone who thinks now that 4 percent is an inflation-safe unemployment rate for the US economy. Jim Tobin mentioned that there has been more discussion about what that number ought to be. Jim's 5.5 percent, which is roughly where I come out as well, is probably a left-wing number. Marty Feldstein ...

Tobin: [interrupting] Thinks we're there now.

Solow: Thinks we're there now – that there is no slack whatever at 6.5 percent unemployment. And there are probably others, including some sitting around this table, who would think that 6 percent is a good number. Okun's floor of 4 percent unemployment has been revised in recent work to something like 5.5 percent or even higher.

Tobin: But I think it may well be that the inflation-safe unemployment rate is below 5.5 percent. The way to approach it is probably to go toward 5.5 percent, and if inflation is still stable or going down, well, you slow down as you get unemployment lower, but you're prepared to go further. That's the way the Volcker recovery went – the recovery that Paul Samuelson talked about. As the economy got closer to what might previously have been thought as the natural rate back in 1980, the Fed was willing to let the unemployment rate drop to 6 percent, and then when that looked pretty good, the Fed went on to 5.5 percent. Now, maybe, given what's happening to oil prices, to labor markets, and so on, that 5.5 percent is too high. We'll find out, and we'll hope the Federal Reserve, independent as it is, will not crack down on the economy just because there is some number they have in mind rather than looking at where they are.

Corden: Do you mean to tell Mr Greenspan what to do? Fiscal policy is ruled out for practical purposes. How do we get to 5.5 percent unemployment? What do we do?

Tobin: What's happened is that the administration is stuck with not having an expansionary fiscal policy. Fiscal policy is frozen for five years, except that it might go in the other direction; there might be even more austerity attempted. Of course something will depend in future years on what happens in medical-care reform. What we may have going, as I think Paul McCracken was suggesting, is a sort of self-perpetuating recovery, in which the momentum will continue for a while, assuming that the Federal Reserve doesn't interrupt it. In the 1960s, the Fed perhaps was not willing to make a dramatic, activist gesture toward easy money to get the economy going, but what it did do was essentially to keep the short-term interest rate constant. It was not leaning against the wind as much as it had usually done in the past. So maybe this time the Fed won't lean against the wind if the inflation outlook is as favorable as it seems to be and if we can proceed with a recovery that doesn't require any additional fiscal stimulus. That's what you've got to hope for if you're Bill Clinton.

Solow: But Max is perfectly right to point out that there is less freedom of action on the part of the administration than there actually is. Fiscal policy is frozen, monetary policy is in the hands of the Fed – fundamentally independent as it is – and that leaves mainly prayer [loud laughter].

Johnson: I don't know whether you realize in the United States how lucky you are when you argue about whether the inflation-safe rate of unemployment is 5.5 or 6.5 percent. We argue about this in Europe; we call it the NAIRU – the non-accelerating inflation rate of unemployment – and the general view is that it's probably between 7 and 8 percent in most major countries. When we lowered our unemployment rate to 5.5 percent, which we briefly did in Britain, we found that inflation rose into double figures. But I think the point about this whole argument is that policy can change the inflation-safe rate of unemployment by the kind of structural labor-market measures that we were discussing this morning. And the drift of the argument in Europe is, why can't we have the kind of labor market they have in America? Let me add that if we wish to achieve price stability in a European monetary union, and if the price of price stability is 7.5 percent unemployment, that's probably not going to be politically acceptable.

I would like to raise one other point and pick up what Jim Tobin was saying about the Clinton health-care reform, which is one of the president's top priorities. I think it does raise the question of how the United States can finance anything like this kind of program without losing all the competitiveness which it has gained, not only with the lower dollar but in various other ways. The main danger is that you finance what seems like a desirable reform – health care for everybody – by loading costs onto employers through higher social-security taxation, and the reaction from Europe would be that almost any other way of financing extra health care is better than that, because it would be an additional tax on jobs. The American non-wage labor–cost ratio is average; it is not particularly low, and therefore it would seem desirable to finance additional health care, if not out of the citizen's purse, then out of general taxation or even by deficit financing if that's what the economy is going to need in future years.

Samuelson: I would like to address the question which Max Corden asked – not to rebut the point but to analyze it. Let's suppose that what is guiding this economy can be well described in primitive Keynesian terms by the IS–LM schedules, and Max's question is, how is it that when we're evaluating one year of Clinton, we can give so much credit to Clinton for the better behavior of the economy when it doesn't appear to be the case that he has moved his little finger against one or the other of those curves? The point I want to make is that we're dealing with political economy, not just economics. When Franklin Roosevelt ran for office in 1932, he ran on a balanced-budget platform. He

later asked his main speech writer to take a week off and justify
what he had been doing in terms of what he had promised to do.
What was his name?

Solow:　Rosenman.

Samuelson:　Yes; Rosenman came back and said, 'There's
only one thing you can do, chief, and that is: deny you ever made
those speeches!' [loud laughter]. However, the American people
were not fooled. They knew which of those two people on the
campaign trail, Herbert Hoover or Franklin Roosevelt, would be
the more ready spender if there came to be a need for ready
spending. And most of them were convinced there was such a
need. This happens repeatedly in American politics. People look
back to General Eisenhower's two terms as a golden age – just as
phonily golden as Calvin Coolidge's age that they look back on.
Now there were three National Bureau recessions tucked into
Eisenhower's two terms. How do I know that? I read it in the
Guinness Book of Records. Also, I was there at the time. So when
John F. Kennedy ran against Richard Nixon during a National
Bureau recession in 1960, and he talked about getting the country moving again – at a time when the Secretary of the Treasury
of the outgoing Eisenhower administration denied there was a
recession – the people knew which of those two candidates would
be the readier spender if it became requisite to do something
about the IS–LM curves.

The same thing happened with George Bush and his rather
dismal plea: 'Let's get capital gains taxes down'. He and his
people kept insisting that the country wasn't as badly off as the
public thought it was. The Bush-inspired view was: 'It's like
Wagner's music; it's not as bad as it sounds'. Well, actually, the
election-day quarter was a very strong quarter for the GNP accounts. The day the Gallup Polls all foretold that Clinton was
going to win, you saw a boost in consumer confidence. Now I
don't believe in consumer confidence as any long-run, important,
exogenous variable in the IS–LM apparatus, but in the short run
those are not exact curves anchored in strong basic reality; they
are very much affected by what people think. And, yes, Clinton
was lucky, but in part it was his kind of program, his kind of

oratory that made his luck. This is all in the short-run accumula-
tor. You can't lean on it in the long run. Herbert Hoover could not
in 1929, after the stock-market crash, say, 'We have nothing to
fear but fear itself; all we have to do is believe in American
capitalism' in order to stem the bank failures and so forth.

Now when Kennedy came in – this is early, before he got an
expensive education from Jim Tobin and Walter Heller,

Tobin: Et al.

Samuelson: He really thought his oratory was going to do
the job – get the country moving ahead. You should have seen the
pained look on his aides' faces to learn that they had to do
something and even to expand something called the deficit.
Kennedy had been elected, and his campaign had come to life
when he asked the American people for sacrifice. And he said,
'Do you want me to ask the American people, as the first sacrifice, to take a tax cut?' Well, that didn't go into effect for many
months, but the National Bureau recession, which was on during
the campaign, ended on February 15, which was only a few days
after Inauguration Day. I was impressed by the power of the new
president to turn things around so quickly. But the Gallup polls
were going in his favor, public confidence was going in his favor
– the things which would make the IS–LM curves better. Even
though we have an independent Federal Reserve, there's a lot of
leaning that can be done in the background; there's a lot of taking
over inside the executive branch of functions which normally are
left to the central bank. And that is a threat that always hangs
over stubborn, recalcitrant, independent central bankers. You can
begin to do the things which were turned over to the Bank of
England by the British government 200 years ago. Those can be
brought back in the way you handle your open-market operations, the way you time veteran benefits, and so forth. So long as
Clinton retains popularity, not all of which he earned, and has an
expansionist leaning, that is an objective factor which I, as a
betting man in office pools on what's going to happen to the
GDP, do take into account. And I think that's what's operating.

Now I completely agree that the health program is a wild
cannon on the deck, because my father taught me, 'Never believe

in a miracle until it happens'. It's hard enough to believe it after it happens. To give coverage to everybody, to do it without an increase in cost to almost anybody, to do it by militant consumer-group bargaining with deep-pocket insurance companies, and to alter the third-party payment system that our own health system is based upon – to bet in advance that this will take place is, to use the familiar expression, to believe in the tooth fairy. We're in a political system which is not going to let the Clinton team get that comprehensive health program in its entirety until there is some clearer indication of what miracles you have to believe in to vote for it. That's all going to be a factor in the next election that we're running ahead toward.

Tobin: I think one thing that is very important is whether people think the Federal Reserve is going to have occasion or reason to raise interest rates. If things happen in a way which makes the general public, especially business people and financial markets, believe that there will not be a tightening of Federal Reserve policy in the coming months, that is itself a stimulus. It's a good thing; it shows up in long-term interest rates, in long-term real rates. That's what's important – not just the fact that long-term nominal rates are lower. In line with what Paul Samuelson has just said, I think that low stable real interest rates can be a positive factor in recovery that may make up for the absence of dollars and cents of fiscal stimulus that we aren't getting.

On the health-care business, I think that already we see that the administration is backing off from a lot of things. For example, they already have an exemption from their program for any employer that has 5,000 or more employees, so those employers can continue their health systems without any interference from what they're doing now. And Secretary Bentsen told the National Association of Manufacturers yesterday that this threshold will be reduced below 5,000 so that even more employers will be able to maintain their self-insured plans unchanged. And they're not subject to any more taxes on what they're doing. So a large number of health plans that already exist will just continue the way they are – won't be interfered with. But I think Paul is right; the employer mandate is the main weakness of the program, for many reasons.

Cooper: I'd like to comment on Paul's remarks about shifting IS and LM curves. I looked up the blue-chip forecasts that were being made just before the election in 1992 to get a base line for what was reasonable to compare against now, and it might be worth mentioning them. The blue-chip forecasters are a group of 52 people who make their living forecasting, and their forecasts are simply averaged every month. The blue-chip forecast just before the election was for a fourth-quarter GDP growth of 2.6 percent, against the 2.8 percent that we actually observed. So there may have been a shift in IS–LM, but it wasn't very big. On inflation as measured by the consumer-price index, the blue-chip forecast was 3.2 percent; this comes in at 2.8 percent, partly due to lower oil prices, thanks to the Europeans and the Japanese. The really big surprise is the unemployment rate, which was forecast at 7.2 percent for November 1993; in that month it was 6.7 percent, and has since come down further. After months of recovery based mainly on productivity growth, with little effect on the unemployment rate, in the last year we have had a sudden spurt of employment growth. And long-term interest rates have come down. The long-term corporate bond rate is 130 basis points below the forecast, but doesn't seem to have provided much stimulus to GNP so far.

Samuelson: As long as you're reporting on empirical experience, it would be useful to report what the University of Michigan and the Conference Board polls show about consumer confidence.

Cooper: You're not talking about a forecast, but just the facts. Those I did look at. Consumer confidence is up 10 points on 100 between October 1992 and the end of 1993.

McCracken: Do you have figures for October to December 1992?

Cooper: Well, what happened to consumer confidence, actually, was a sharp rise after the election, then a big fall in the first half of 1993 followed by a big rise in the second half and ending up 10 points higher than the year before – but with a big U-shape in the meantime.

Solomon: I would like to raise a longer-term question based on Jim Tobin's observations about US productivity growth, and ask him to disaggregate that a bit. We know, if I'm not mistaken, that in manufacturing, productivity growth was quite rapid during this period. Are we measuring productivity in services adequately and therefore measuring total productivity growth adequately?

Tobin: Productivity in manufacturing has been doing well for several years.

Solomon: All through the 1980s, I think.

Tobin: Yes, manufacturing is 20 percent of GDP, so it's not a big factor in the labor force; 16 percent of the labor force is in manufacturing.

Solow: Part of the growth in productivity is because the labor force is being well-behaved. It's worthwhile mentioning here something that Lionel McKenzie mentioned earlier. Zvi Griliches pointed out in his presidential address at the American Economic Association that the growth of productivity in manufacturing and in a few other sectors for which we think we measure productivity reasonably accurately has not decelerated very much, if at all. I think there has been some deceleration in manufacturing, whereas the sectors where measured productivity has decelerated turn out to be the sectors where we think the measurement is rather bad – that the errors, even the conceptual errors, are quite large. But there's not much reason to suppose that sectors with poorly measured or poorly defined productivity should be biased in the direction of very slow growth – why the errors should be more in that direction now than they were in the years between 1950 and 1970. It's a reminder that there's more going on here than we know about.

McCracken: And that sector has grown.

Solow: Yes – services.

Cooper: And that dominates the measurement; 80 percent of the labor force is in areas that we measure poorly. I'd like to remind the people around the table that in the national accounts the productivity growth for teachers is entered as zero.

Solow: Zero.

Cooper: So that as a higher and higher fraction of the labor force become teachers, with everything else the same, measured aggregate productivity growth declines.

Solow: But that's not fair. Serious people who talk about productivity exclude from even the aggregate the output generated by government, where the productivity increase is defined as zero, as well as the output generated by the imputed value of the services of houses and things like that, where the productivity numbers simply make no sense.

Samuelson: Except in education, where we know it's true [laughter].

McKenzie: I knew somebody was going to say that!

Mundell: Well, since Paul Samuelson wants to rule out the 1920s as a good period – that was Calvin Coolidge's period; we shouldn't sing to that – there have really been only two decades in this century that were good ones: the 1960s and the 1980s in some sense. Of course the second decade was a war period, and we rule out the 1920s, the Roaring Twenties, because that was Calvin Coolidge's decade.

Samuelson: I withdraw my remark; it was unworthy of me. Calvin Coolidge was very lucky, and we were lucky with him.

Mundell: Right, good, okay. But the 1930s was a dreadful decade, the 1940s were war years, and the 1950s were the Eisenhower years; we have to rule those out too, because Paul said so.

Samuelson: They're in the *Guinness Book of Records*.

Mundell: Okay, because of the three recessions. But it wasn't really all that bad a period; it was a period of stable prices with a lot of good points in terms of the Okun misery index. It was a good period.

Samuelson: Well, in the 1950s, if you were engaged as I was in the growth sweepstakes business, you would find that the 1950s was not a good period.

Mundell: I'm judging it by the subsequent periods.

Solow: Bob, what looks to you like stable prices was complained about all through the 1950s under the name 'creeping inflation'.

Mundell: Oh, I know; I lived through that decade too. We thought the inflation was terrible; it was 2.5 or 3 percent. We didn't like it. But the later decades were of course much worse.

The 1970s was a really terrible decade with rampant inflation, but the 1980s got us back on the track. So we've had two good decades: the 1960s, except for the Vietnam War, and the 1980s. In both of them a very important source of stimulus in generating growth in the economy were the tax cuts – the Kennedy–Johnson tax cut in 1964 and the Reagan tax cut in 1981. In those two really good decades in this century, the tax cuts played a key role. What's happening in the 1990s? The present decade started out rather badly, with the recession commencing in the middle of 1990, and Bush certainly will go down as one of the unluckiest presidents in modern times.

Tobin: The 1980s look good if you start on January 1, 1983. The first three years weren't so great!

Mundell: But remember, a high cost had to be paid temporarily for stopping a 15 percent a year inflation.

Tobin: Whatever the reason, that's another matter.

Mundell: In any case, this was the longest or second longest expansion on record: from November 1982 until July 1990. And you can fight about whether that beats or doesn't beat the Kennedy–Johnson expansion period, but they're about equal, depending on how you measure them.

Tobin: They're equal in the way that 80 equals 100.

Mundell: Well, it depends on what measure you're using. But what I'm arguing is that toward the end of 1995 this expansion, if it's still continuing at that time, is going to be sixteen to eighteen quarters old. The favorable factors in the economy from now through the 1990s are a low dollar – and that makes America very competitive – and low oil prices, but that helps Japan and Europe more than it helps the United States. However, there's going to be this nagging effect from the Clinton medical program. America spends more on health than any other country in the world – about 15 percent of GDP. And when the medical plan takes effect, I think it very unlikely that that's not going to increase health expenditures. Most people I've talked to who know something about this think that the medical plan is going to raise health costs to something like 18 percent of GDP.

Now that's going to be a drag on the economy. If almost 20 percent of the economy has to be taken up in medical spending, this is going to cut into investment, expansion and job growth in other sectors. Of course there is some improvement in housing, but I don't think that housing is going to be a major stimulus in the 1990s. The automobile industry is doing great now, but there's an inventory cycle which goes with that, and I'm sure we're not going to have more than two years of really strong automobile production.

Samuelson: Is this the Mundell Doctrine of Secular Stagnation?

Mundell: I've argued something else – that there's a demographic factor operating in this connection. It does seem to me that the economy is going to be in trouble, and I think the people who are advising Clinton really need to find a contingency plan in the event that there is a recession in 1995. I think myself that the Clinton administration in its own interest should, at the very minimum, index – and I would prefer also to cut – the capital-gains tax. In my judgment, that would have a very favorable effect on the US economy.

Wakatsuki: I am wondering whether this pattern of recovery in the United States will occur in Europe and Japan as well. The reduction in US unemployment is much bigger than expected and than most economists had forecasted. But the quality of employment is shifting from the manufacturing sector to the nonmanufacturing sector, and I assume that the quality of job is not necessarily to the satisfaction of many people. That might mean that the United States is not immune from the same phenomenon from which Europe is suffering. Perhaps this pattern of recovery could be repeated in Europe, and that would mean that most of the recovery in employment would come in the service-oriented sector. This might be the case in Japan after our slump is over, the manufacturing sector becoming much leaner while the service-oriented sectors, which are not so productive and perhaps lower paid, are expanding. And I'm wondering whether the US pattern of recovery is an aberration or whether something new is going on.

Cooper: On the question of employment, we always have cycles and secular trends. In my view, to put it oversimply, manufacturing is going the way that agriculture has gone. We never mention agriculture, but agriculture historically has had, and continues to have, the most rapid growth of labor productivity of any sector. My guess is that employment in manufacturing will continue to decline in the United States. We have a strong automobile year, we may get some increase there, but it's against the secular decline. And Europe and Japan will experience the same trend.

Now the way Mr Wakatsuki put the question suggested that this was a bad thing. I have exactly the contrary view. I don't know about the shop floor in Japan; maybe it's a lot better than here, but most manufacturing jobs in the United States are awful, and the faster we get rid of them from a social point of view, the better. Now the complaint is often made that workers go from a high-paid steel-making job to a low-paid hamburger-pushing job. It's true that we have a lot of low-paying service jobs, but we have a lot of high-paying service jobs also, and it is a mistake to think of service jobs as typically being low-quality, low-paying jobs. Let me point out that all the people in this room are in the service industry.

The most rapidly growing component of the US labor force, as we measure it, is in the category 'Other other services'. These are jobs of the future which are too unimportant today to be separately identified. They of course start small, but they are the ones that are growing the most rapidly. The entire computer software industry was in 'Other other services' ten years ago, as well as much of the biotech industry, which is not yet manufacturing but may at some point become manufacturing. So we should not fall into the habit of thinking that reduction in manufacturing jobs and shifting to the service sector is a movement against social welfare.

Samuelson: Hear, hear!

7. Maastricht and the Issue of European Monetary Union

Introduced by Christopher Johnson

Chairman Cooper: I thought this morning we would turn to the more explicitly international issues. The items suggested for our agenda in yesterday morning's discussion included European monetary developments, and I propose that we start out with that topic, with Christopher Johnson leading the discussion. So if that's agreeable, I shall turn the floor over to Christopher.

Johnson: Well, I hope I'm speaking as a European, and of course we British are in Europe. However, some of my compatriots have a slightly eccentric view on this matter, and I shall try to express a European view rather than a purely British one.

Now I want to sketch in a bit of background for the benefit of those to whom EMU may be the kind of bird you see when you go on a package tour in Australia. I want first to remind us of what the reasons are why Europe is going through what may seem like the most extraordinary contortions. First of all, we want to end the damaging effects of exchange-rate fluctuations. Secondly, we went to complete the single European market for goods, services and capital by having a single currency that will give us a single set of prices. Many people believe that this is necessary to achieve full integration of the market. We want to ensure a regime of stable prices, and this is logically separate from what I've said about having a single currency. A single currency is by no means synonymous with stable prices, but we want to have a good single currency which doesn't lose its value and will thus be an improvement on what has prevailed in the majority of European member countries.

Finally, there is an important political motive, which is to link Germany into the European system. This now becomes more important than ever with the end of the Cold War and the temptations for the Germans to look eastward. Now the mechanism for this process is one on which Paul Samuelson has poured a certain amount of cold water: the Maastricht Treaty. Well, I would say that the Maastricht Treaty is like the US Constitution; it's what the founding fathers have handed us. We might not start from here if we had it to do all over again, but it's the document that everybody has agreed on. It has lots of loopholes and possibilities of interpretation. But as somebody said about Stravinsky's music, it's not as bad as it sounds.

Samuelson: That was said about Wagner.

Johnson: Not Stravinsky?

Samuelson: No, Wagner.

Johnson: Wagner; sorry. But I never believed that about Wagner. Now the Maastricht Treaty provides for a kind of three-stage rocket mechanism, and I'll describe what those stages are in a minute. But it's like a rocket in that when you've been through each stage, you drop off that stage of the rocket, and the next stage is different. And, most important, the Maastricht Treaty lays down criteria for economic convergence, and I shall go through what those are and see how near we are to achieving them.

Now the three stages. Stage One is, in effect, the old EMS – the European Monetary System – and it's assumed that all countries joined, which they all did except Greece. They didn't all stay in, but they joined for a time. And we also achieved free capital movements, which has important implications for the way we run the system if we don't want to abandon that achievement.

Stage Two started on the first day of this month [January 1994], so it's something new and rather exciting. It's a stage from the EMS to the single currency. The main feature is the establishment of the European Monetary Institute, which will be in Frankfurt but which is still in Basle, where it is in fact wearing its new hats by the Committee of Central Bank Governors, and it is going to be run by Alexandre Lamfalussy, who has been running the Bank for International Settlements. Now the EMI will have no power to run a single monetary policy. Countries still retain charge of their own monetary policy, but they agree to cooperate in the EMI, which also has important functions in monitoring the exchange-rate mechanism and promoting the ecu. And we also have a new exercise in policy coordination done through the Economic and Financial Council – ECOFIN. Governments are still in charge of fiscal and other economic policy, but they agree to cooperate in achieving the convergence programs.

Then the final stage, Stage Three, is when we shall get a European central bank as part of the European system incorporating the national central banks. It will start perhaps at the beginning of 1997 – well, that's according to the treaty anyway – but to begin with, it will mean that exchange rates are irrevocably fixed. It will take about five years from the point of decision to bring a single currency into full operation.

Now I want to talk about the convergence criteria which are the key to Stage Two that we've embarked on and which are in most people's view a precondition of monetary union. It would be possible, of course, to create a monetary union tomorrow, as happened between East and West Germany, but it would be extremely difficult and disruptive. Of course the first and most important convergence criterion is that exchange rates should converge, and many people think that because the ERM, the exchange-rate mechanism, has broken down, that means the end of EMU, European Monetary Union. I want to show that this is not so at all. The ERM that we had was an unstable equilibrium. For five years, there were no changes in exchange rates. The ERM was unstable because countries were using fixed exchange rates to get inflation down. This was very successful but, as a result, countries were left with overvalued exchange rates because they were accumulating past inflation which they were not able to purge without either leaving the ERM or devaluing, which of course is what happened. In September 1992, Britain and Italy left the ERM, and subsequently Spain, Portugal and Ireland devalued.

Now this was in fact a blessing in disguise, because it left us with a much more stable long-run set of exchange rates. If we assume that inflation rates remain as low as they are now, we have a much better starting point for monetary union than we had before. However, this wasn't enough to forestall the second crisis in August 1993, and that was really due not to the exchange rates being misaligned but to the conflicting monetary objectives, particularly between Germany, on the one hand, and France and other countries, on the other. And it was because the market believed that since the other countries, which were worried about unemployment, could not keep their interest rates as high as German rates, the system was bound to break up and that countries which wanted lower interest rates would have to devalue.

The solution adopted – wide bands of 15 percent – really means a change not just in quantity but in quality from the previous ERM, which had 2.5 percent bands for most members. However, the arrangement has been very successful in that the stronger currencies, like the French franc, have moved de facto backward to the old narrow bands, because their fundamentals are sound and they no longer provide a target for speculators. The need to introduce a 'Tobin tax', as Jim has often advocated, now seems much less. And many people are prepared now to accept wider bands and to devise some perhaps more meaningful tests for exchange-rate stability, such as low volatility around a stable mean. So exchange-rate convergence, I think, is still perfectly possible. It's perhaps not the most important form of convergence, because once you have a single currency, then exchange rates don't matter anymore.

The next important criterion is inflation convergence. Clearly, if you're aiming at price stability, you want to start from a position of low inflation and, in fact, this has been practically achieved. Eight out of twelve countries now have inflation within the prescribed limits. One may say that this is an unfair test because we're in a recession, but of course one does have to hope that inflation won't rise in the recovery and that steps will be taken to avoid that. However, the problem with inflation is that the price paid to get it down has been too high. There has been too much emphasis on monetary policy and high interest rates, and therefore there is a general mood, not least among the people who are going to run the new central bank, that some of the load should be taken off monetary policy and that there should be more convergence of labour markets and of unemployment rates, of course in a downward direction. Otherwise, the price paid to keep inflation down will make the whole enterprise not worthwhile. I won't say much about long-term interest rates, because inflation and inflation expectations are low. Long-term interest rates have, in fact, converged in most countries, and the bottom figure is about 5.5 percent. Most countries are between that and 7.5 percent. And this of course is one of the other aims of the EMU – to have low interest rates over a wide area to stimulate investment.

Now the criterion which will be most difficult to achieve is that of restricting budget deficits to 3 percent of GDP. Many economists have poked fun at this fiscal numerology of Maastricht, and it is very much a rough-and-ready rule of thumb. There are enough exceptions in the wording to allow countries which achieve a fiscally responsible position to exceed the limit if they have a deficit due to investment in infrastructure or due to a recession. The point about deficits which is often overlooked is that they are extremely volatile cyclically. We had, in fact, convergence of deficits in most countries in the late 1980s in the boom; now there is no country which is down to 3 percent except Luxembourg, but by the time recovery comes in 1995 or '96, we should see most of these deficits tracking down again toward 3 percent simply because of the cyclical effect.

And somebody will surely say these deficits are structural. The structural part is getting worse, but most countries have plans to tackle that as well. The era of pretending that tax cuts are always good in every circumstance, politically and economically – that heresy of the 1980s – I think people have now turned against. So I think there is much more chance than one might now believe that deficits will converge. Debt–GDP ratios are more difficult, but they're not quite so important under the treaty. About half the countries are over the 60 percent limit, but the important thing about this is that the ratio should be stable or, better still, falling. Sustainability is usually interpreted as meaning a stable debt–

GDP ratio, but in too many cases the ratio is rising, which is a mathematical consequence of having a temporarily large deficit; the debt–GDP ratio tends to rise when the cycle is down and to fall when it's up.

I want to conclude by saying in rather more concrete terms what the prospects are, which countries will go ahead, and when. The first date for decision is 1996, and I think that because of the timing of the business cycle, 1996 could be quite a good year for convergence. Some countries one could regard as almost certain to be observing the criteria by then. Germany has had problems, but is getting inflation down, and the deficit is going to stabilize in France, Luxembourg and the Netherlands. And then there's another group of countries which are probable or possible but not certain candidates. Belgium and Italy have deficit and debt problems. Spain and Portugal still have quite high inflation. Ireland has a high debt, but might still qualify on other counts. One can count out Greece, which won't be ready.

Two of the key countries which could decide this whole thing are the UK and Denmark, which look as though they will in fact achieve the convergence criteria, but they have both said that they may opt out of monetary union. If so, they won't be in it, and their votes won't count. We need a majority of seven out of twelve countries if we're to go ahead in 1996. As you've seen, there are four almost certain ones. If three out of the five doubtfuls, or one or two out of the optional ones decide to come in, we could well have a decision to go ahead in 1996. If not, then in 1998 – that is the next time there will be a decision – and then we don't even need a majority of countries. We could have a narrow monetary union or a two-speed union, which many people advocate, so that countries which were ready could go ahead; the others could join them later.

There are dangers in that. It could be disruptive. Countries which get left out of the first wave could deteriorate because of lack of market confidence and support, so I think there is considerable advantage in having as many countries going ahead as possible. And this also, of course, would bring a great advantage; the more countries using a single currency, the greater the advantage to one and all. Clearly, the scope of monetary union is one of the important advantages to offset against the once-for-all transition costs which undoubtedly will be incurred.

Now my conclusion would be that the whole thing in fact depends on the political decision by the key countries – most of all by Germany. If the Germans want to go ahead even as soon as 1996, they will find ways of interpreting the treaty. The German government will if necessary find ways of overruling the Bundesbank, which has considerable reservations, just as the government did at the time of German monetary union. Exchange rates and monetary union are matters for political decisions by governments, and whether Germany wants to go ahead will depend on domestic politics. There is already a party whose main plank seems to be: defend the D-Mark against all comers. Let's hope that's a minority view. But the Germans will certainly want a quid pro quo in terms of political union, though not a full federal state – we still envisage independent nation states – but political institutions like the European Parliament, the central bank, the European Council, which will give Germany a degree of political integration to accompany the economic integration. In my view, it would be very dangerous for other countries to pass up any opportunity to bind Germany into the European structure if it looks possible in 1996. It would be dangerous to wait until 1998 or even later. I think what's happening now in Russia may well make people reflect that the reason for starting the whole European integration enterprise arose out of the First and Second World Wars and that whatever one thinks of the economic arguments, which I believe are quite compelling, there is also an overriding political argument why Europe needs to go ahead – with the support, we hope, of the United States.

Cooper: Christopher, before I invite other comments, I have just one technical question: is there agreement on how budget deficits are to be defined? In particular, is it cricket to include asset sales as receipts? What prompts the question is that I notice in recent years that the German budget deficit has been between 3 and 4 percent of GNP – high by German standards but nonetheless moderate. But the German public sector borrowing requirement, including a number of things that are outside of the formal budget, has been over 7 percent of GNP. So this question of definition actually makes quite a difference. How much scope for fudging do the European countries have in getting below the 3 percent.

Johnson: Well, on that particular point, we don't need to fudge, because it's quite clear that the deficits referred to are general government deficits, and therefore they exclude public-sector deficits on the ground that these really depend on how much of your industry is in public hands. A country that happens to have more public ownership is going to have a bigger non-government public-sector deficit if its industries are borrowing heavily. So, fortunately, this means that the German general government deficit is well within sight of 3 percent, and we don't need to worry about the public-sector deficit, which I think is temporary anyway.

Cooper: But just to pursue the point one step further, we had a savings-and-loan crisis in this country. We consolidate our federal deficit, and therefore it has included all of the cash flow associated with the S and L bailout. Germany has a situation in which all the details are different but which in rough terms is analogous. It has done a lot of borrowing on the capital market, and that's outside the German budget; the S and L crisis is inside the US budget. One can argue either; it depends on what purpose you are using the budget deficit for. But if you allow flexibility, it seems to me almost certain that the Europeans will find some way to get within the budget criterion.

Johnson: Yes, I think the answer is probably to exclude financial transactions in both directions. Nobody has done that yet, because it would have the unfortunate effect of excluding the results of privatization sales in countries like Britain and Italy, so I think this is something the statisticians are going to need to argue about quite a lot – and perhaps not just the statisticians.

Cooper: Bob Solomon wants to come in on just this point.

Solomon: I was going to ask about the privatization receipts in particular. We're in a situation in Europe now where, oddly enough, one of the motivations for privatization, which most of us probably think is a good thing, is to bring revenue into the treasury. The French are doing it, and the British have done it since Margaret Thatcher came into office. If I'm not mistaken, the British budgetary figures include privatization receipts as part of government revenues, and therefore don't they reduce the budget deficit?

Johnson: Well, they reduce the budget deficit, but because they're subtracted from expenditure rather than being added to revenue.

Cooper: Well, I'm glad I got that straight! [loud laughter]

Solomon: I'm just going to repeat this question: in determining whether a country meets the convergence criterion, may that country include privatization receipts or not – either to reduce budget expenditure or to increase revenues?

Johnson: Well, that has yet to be decided. I would just make the point that once you have privatized what you can privatize, it makes very little difference to the long-term sustainability of the fiscal position. I think allowance will be made for this in some way but, strictly speaking, it seems to me to fall outside the criterion as originally envisaged. However, I've no doubt that governments will be capable of making a decision to include privatization receipts if that makes, for example, the Italian deficit look better when it matters.

Jeffrey A. Frankel: I'm sorry I couldn't be here yesterday, but I had to teach a rather large class. I run the risk of saying things that have already been covered, but I'll have to face that danger. What I'm going to say now about European monetary union also runs the danger, from the viewpoint of the European, of being rather rude. I think it's great when a group of countries want to get together and integrate in all kinds of dimensions, including the monetary dimension, and when somebody from the outside says it's not going to work, there's always the possibility that this may sound like one doesn't want it to work, which is not the case. There is a bit of a split here, I think, between American economists and European economists on whether Maastricht and European monetary union can work.

I believe that Maastricht is dead, and until the European leaders acknowledge this fact, it's going to postpone the ultimate date when European monetary integration is possible. Christopher Johnson gave us a very good list of the four advantages of monetary union, and I'll accept those completely, but of course there are disadvantages also – in particular, each country has to give up monetary autonomy. We learned from Bob Mundell years ago about optimum currency areas, and I would list four criteria for when the advantages of a common currency outweigh the disadvantages and it's therefore time to undertake monetary integration. The four criteria are, first, the degree of openness and economic integration of the countries, including labor mobility but especially trade; second, the degree of correlation of macroeconomic disturbances among the countries; third, the extent of common objectives – for example, the weight placed on inflation versus unemployment; and fourth, the degree of political willingness to sacrifice a bit for the cause of a common monetary union.

All four criteria, I think, are moving in the right direction for Europe; Western Europe as a group comes closer to satisfying all criteria than in the past. And I think and hope that the day is not too far off when the criteria are satisfied. But I don't think they are satisfied yet, and I don't think they will be satisfied in 1996 or in 1998. Quite a few economists have said after the crisis in the exchange-rate mechanism of September 1992 that we could have predicted it would happen – that you can't have completely open capital markets, fixed exchange rates and monetary independence all at the same time, and if you try, the arrangement is going to collapse. I think that's basically right, but there's a sort of split as to what went wrong. The inclination among Europeans is to take Maastricht as given, as Christopher Johnson did, and to assume that it is a necessity that they go forward and try to decide how best to do it.

One common view is that the problem has been the attempt to go through three stages and that you can't do this; you have to jump directly to Stage Three. The analogy is that you can't cross a chasm in two jumps or three jumps; you have to jump all the way across. Well, I would answer that there are some chasms that are too wide to cross by jumping at all. Perhaps a better analogy is a stream. There are some streams that could possibly be jumped across in a single jump and, if so, you want to get a running start and have enough conviction and momentum. However, there are other streams that are just too wide to cross in a single jump but that can be crossed gradually by looking for the stepping stones, and I think that stages are a necessary part of the road to European monetary union.

On another matter, a recent paper raised the question: where do these fiscal criteria come from in the Maastricht agreement? We understand the exchange-rate criterion, the inflation criterion; they are directly relevant to the question of whether the countries are ready to have a common currency, but where on earth do these fiscal criteria come from? They don't seem directly relevant. The answer I sort of like is that it's an arbitrary test of will.

I would say that Europe is fortunate that the major shock of German monetary union came along when it did rather than at Stage Three. People say that the German shock is a one-time event, but it is not a once in a lifetime sort of event; there will be other shocks of that order of magnitude. In 1996 and 1998, there may be no major shocks, and conditions are likely to be more favorable, except in one dimension, and that is the degree of credibility that the system has among the financial markets and speculators. In 1990, when the last capital controls were removed among European countries, the European exchange-rate mechanism – the ERM – had a very high amount of credibility by virtue of the fact that there had not been a realignment in five years, and in my view it's that cumulative credibility that allowed the ERM to last another two years. That credibility is no longer there – not after September 1992 and especially after the events of last summer [1993]. The system is very fragile, and that's a disadvantage that will be there in 1996 and will be there in 1998 and I think will be there until the Europeans go back to the drawing boards some time early in the next century.

Johnson: Could I just have a two-hander on that, Dick? I think planning for shocks is a bit like living with earthquakes in Los Angeles. You may know in theory that one is likely to happen again sometime, but you never know where or when, so you don't waste too much time replanning everything else around it.

On another matter raised by Jeffrey, let me explain that the reason for limiting budget deficits in what looks like an arbitrary manner is that central bankers, who devised this whole blueprint, are terrified that one or two things will happen: either deficits will be financed by printing money if they're too large or they'll be financed by issuing bonds, which will drive up the long-term interest rate. Either way, one of the other key objectives of monetary union will be jeopardized. And I suppose having the limit at 3 percent of GDP in each country is just like saying that we can have so much of a deficit for the whole area, and we have to share it fairly, so let's do it in proportion to each country's GDP. That's not an economist's argument; it's a kind of political policy-maker's argument.

Willett: I'd like to second Jeff Frankel's comments. My sense is that very few of the studies that try to look at the economic case for monetary integration for the whole group of Western European countries support the view that they're anywhere close to being an optimum currency area. It may make perfect sense, say, for Austria and the Netherlands to integrate with Germany monetarily, but it does not make sense for the whole group. Christopher quite appropriately raised the political issue, because I think he's certainly right that this is primarily a political and not an economic issue. But it's very difficult, I think, to do a careful analysis, because my impression is that the political and economic benefits from trade and economic integration thus far achieved have been tremendous. However, it's a very different question whether you would get substantial additional benefits by moving on to full monetary unification. I think we need to do a much more differentiated analysis to learn what would be the additional political costs and benefits – not just the economic costs and benefits – of going forward.

I would like to close by moving the discussion back to yesterday's remarks by Paul Samuelson, who made some critical comments about Maastricht, half of which I strongly agreed with; the other half I strongly disagreed with. His argument was, look, Maastricht is dead, which I think may be true in a sense, but it has left a legacy of forcing countries like France to move to an independent central bank. Well, I happen to be strongly in favor of independent central banks. One striking fact is that when you look across the industrial countries, the more independent central banks tend to have substantially lower rates of inflation, and this occurs without a cost in terms of lower growth. The independence need not be absolute. There are a number of fascinating experiments, of which the New Zealand case is the one I'm particularly attracted to, because it presents an interesting compromise between complete independence and complete subjection to the government. The basic idea is that you negotiate contracts between the central bank and the government, and then the central bank is held responsible for meeting those contracts. The contracts don't have to specify price stability at all costs, a matter which was concerning Paul Samuelson and others yesterday. Let me just end with a question to Christopher: what is the current state of debate about independence for the Bank of England?

Johnson: I'll answer that very briefly if I may. There has recently been a report of the Treasury Select Committee of the House of Commons, to which I was an adviser, recommending a greater degree of independence for the Bank of England, rather on the New Zealand model, so that the government would have an ultimate override, but would have to be seen to exercise it in the context for that. But the government itself has not accepted the report. It has given the Bank of England a very limited degree of independence because, politically, the Chancellor of the Exchequer prefers to keep control of interest rates. The policy is in fact that the Chancellor and the Governor of the Bank decide at a monthly meeting whether or not to have a change in interest rates, and the Bank's independence has been rather unkindly caricatured as the Chancellor saying, 'Okay, Governor, you can choose the time for the change; any time between 9:00 and 9:15 this morning will do!'. In fact, the Governor has the discretion any time within the following month to carry out the change in what seems like the best moment.

Tobin: I really don't understand at all the argument for deficit–GNP convergence. If there were a ratio that was somewhat more relevant, it would be the government deficit in relation to the saving of the country. That would permit Japan as a big-saving economy to have bigger budget deficits as a percentage of GNP than a low-saving economy like the United States. In any case, if we observe the currency union in which we are living right now, we don't have any such restrictions in our national Constitution on the fiscal policies of the member states. They can diverge in their policies from some of the crazinesses of California to very different policies in other states.

If you look at what makes things work in the United States – in this federation – one of the big things is labor mobility, so that one of the big adjustments to shocks is that people can move easily, and do, from one state to another, from one region to another. And another thing: if California has an earthquake, it gets $6.6 billion, because that was the size of the earthquake. That sort of assistance is taken for granted; when California has an earthquake, when the midwest has a flood, or when Florida has a hurricane, there is an understanding that the whole union comes to the rescue. That doesn't seem to be a part of the Maastricht agreement – that the luckier member countries are going to help the unlucky countries from various kinds of shocks; not just natural disasters, but economic difficulties as well.

Finally, I do have the feeling that the whole spirit of the treaty is to solidify and put into the constitution a kind of austere price stability – exclusively – instead of dealing with the economic problems that Europe is suffering from right now.

Solomon: Just a question to Christopher. I assume the convergence criteria are simply qualifications for joining the monetary union. What are the rules, if any, on fiscal policy once the EMU comes into existence? We know that member countries will not have an independent monetary policy.

Johnson: The fiscal-policy criteria are the only ones which are meant to be permanent. The others are simply hurdles before you get in, but they become irrelevant after that.

Solomon: Yes, but what are the rules?

Johnson: Well, the same – the 3 percent limit except in certain circumstances.

Solomon: The same limit applies even after monetary union?

Johnson: Yes.

Solomon: There's been a fair amount of literature on how countries in the EMU will deal with country-specific shocks when they don't have an independent monetary policy. People have written articles about how in the United States we have a fairly large amount of transfer from the federal government through unemployment compensation and the taxation system that at least partially offsets cyclical differences among the states. The central budget will be much, much smaller in Europe than it is in the United States, and you will not have that sort of built-in stabilizer effects from the federal to the state level. How do country-specific shocks get dealt with?

Johnson: Well, there's no doubt that for the kind of shock you might have in mind, it would mean that the country's budget deficit would increase, but the rules are designed to allow for a deficit to increase under the pressure of a shock, which would happen automatically because there would be less tax revenue coming in and more welfare payments going out. So you could, in fact, have a degree of automatic stabilization even without aid from the center. But this is an answer also to Jim Tobin. There is provision for the so-called structural funds, which means there is some aid from the center. It's meant mainly for the lower-income countries to enable them to deal with the problems of transition, but the funds have also been used for natural disasters – an earthquake in Italy or a mine disaster in the UK. Money is actually paid from the Commission's budget.

But I would like to make another point in response to Jim. I fully sympathize with his criterion about the national saving ratio being important. But of course you have to look at the saving and investment expenditure of each sector, not only the public sector. Even more important, the whole concept of national saving in a single financial market with unrestricted capital flows becomes obsolete, because the citizens of each country will be free to invest their savings wherever they think the return will be best. The Italians could invest their savings in Germany, but this would not justify a big Italian budget deficit.

Tobin: Presumably, what you want to avoid is that the Italians are going to cause interest rates to rise in the whole area, so it is relevant whether it's the actions of one country or another that puts such pressures on the community-wide capital markets. Right? Otherwise, one might just say that since these things affect the capital markets, the discipline of those markets takes care of the whole matter, and you don't have to worry about it. The profligate government is not going to want to increase its interest payments by borrowing in a market like that. I assume that the market will have differential interest rates as between Spain and Germany, for example.

Johnson: That is a very interesting controversy. Will market discipline, in putting lower ratings on Italian debt, be enough of a disincentive to Italy to run deficits? And the answer is almost certainly no; market discipline is not enough in such cases. Countries which are desperate are often quite happy to pay a few hundred extra basis points to finance their expenditure.

Tobin: Well, when New York City was desperately putting burdens of that kind on the capital market, the capital market just shut down lending to it, and maybe that would happen in Europe too. That could be more effective than just the higher interest rate.

Johnson: That actually happens under the Maastricht Treaty. One sanction is that a country can be officially prevented from borrowing in the capital markets in case the markets don't shut down of their own accord.

Samuelson: I want to discuss the truly scientific question of how Maastricht will work out and what is feasible. I will start by saying that a system of pegged exchange rates can work, and can work for a long time. After all, the gold standard was itself such a system, and most of the time in the nineteenth century it did work. And the nineteenth century was a fairly tumultuous time. I think I could give the following classroom assignment: prove and develop the argument whether a *laissez-faire* economy will adjust better to a pegged exchange-rate regime than mixed economies. And I think I would give the highest grades to those who proved that a pegged-rate regime will work better for a *laissez-faire* world, because in a *laissez-faire* world there would not be the discretion for anybody to deviate from the rules of the game.

Now it may well be that this is exactly what's in back of Tom Willett's mind. I know it's in Gottfried Haberler's screeds all the time – to restore the pre-interventionist world. But whether you want a completely *laissez-faire* economy or a more *laissez-faire* economy or a less *laissez-faire* economy, in the real world you are going to have a mixture of variously mixed economies. The result is that when you try to put Humpty Dumpty back together again, it's not going to stay back together again. It's going to breathe through its loopholes, which are the periodic changes in exchange rates.

This was the alleged advantage of the gold standard. Under the gold standard, you readjusted currencies once in eternity; under Bretton Woods, you did it once every fifteen years or once every seventeen years. Now what bothers me – and here my friendship in the underworld of traders and speculators influences me – if the thing were to be done, 'twere well it were done yesterday. You are setting up periods of time in which it is pretty clear to the speculators which way the next exchange-rate change is going to go. And you spend the taxpayer's money lavishly to buy three weeks of time, to buy five weeks of time; as Talleyrand would say, it's worse than a crime, it's a blunder. I don't have any philosophical objections, as the late Dr Hayek might have, to intervention; I just think it's generally a mistake. It's done by stupid people who give win–win situations to nimble people.

So now we're going to have an experiment with European pegged currencies. It's going to have its good period and then its bad period. The reason I think it will run into a bad period is that the market-clearing real wage ratios are going to change in Europe over time. A Portugal develops more rapidly than Greece, a France does better or does worse. We keep bringing up earthquakes; if you have lots of little earthquakes, I understand that this is better, because you're releasing the accumulated tensions and you don't have the big one. I think the floating exchange-rate regime has served the US, for example, very well. Mostly, the changes in rates have been in the direction of what economic law would suggest retroactively. I meet people who say, 'Intervene now', but whose advice is not followed; when I meet them again the next year, they admit that intervention would have been a dreadful mistake, but then they say, 'Now you should intervene!'.

I wouldn't go back to the barbaric relic of gold, and I don't like the view of the guy who says, 'I've got a gold standard proposal without gold'. He's got all of the difficulties still operating in that system except the coolie labor that goes into the mines.

Corden: I have the impression that the Maastricht Treaty presents a tremendous ambiguity. On the one hand, there is a target – an intention to move to monetary union – and then conditions are set up, the convergence conditions, which I won't say make it impossible to get to the target, but indicate a certain lack of desire to get there. Now as I understand it, the story is this: basically, France, Italy and the Benelux countries want monetary union, and the Germans are uncomfortable. One reason is that the Germans already have the Deutsche Mark; they don't need anything else. So to please the Germans, to satisfy the Germans, those convergence conditions were developed which are very demanding – so much so that it may be almost impossible to reach the target. That seems to me the underlying sort of situation.

Now the question is, what is actually likely to happen? Well, the only thing that's feasible, I would have thought, is a two-speed arrangement, where one group achieves monetary union and the other countries possibly never join, or not for a long time. The countries forming the union would be, above all, France and Germany, with the Benelux people delighted to join them, and presumably Austria and possibly Italy, but that's more questionable.

I've asked myself, what considerations are likely to be crucial when the time comes? Now the formal convergence conditions will not be fulfilled, but since they are really very flexible when you look at them carefully, they can be circumvented; there are elements of flexibility there. The budgetary requirements, I gather, offer considerable flexibility. The original exchange-rate condition was that exchange rates were going to stay for two years within the narrow margins. Well, there aren't any narrow margins anymore. The margins are now so wide that in fact there is a managed floating exchange-rate system for all practical purposes.

So I think the countries can formally get around the convergence conditions. The question is, will they want to move ahead when the time comes? Well, I think there are three considerations. First of all, if the economies are in a state of boom at the time, then it's more likely that they will move on schedule. On the other hand, if the big step is postponed, then there may be another recession. We know we have recessions, and if there's a recession, then people will be more reluctant. The third consideration that I think is very important is the rise of nationalism and the increasing votes for the right-wing minority parties. Now the stronger this nationalistic or fascist or right-wing movement becomes, particularly in France and Germany, the more pressure there will be, first of all, for Keynesian kinds of policy to remove unemployment and, secondly, more resentment of getting into something that will involve foreigners partly deciding crucial policies. The Germans would be more reluctant to give up the Deutsche Mark, and the French would resist a central bank that would be dominated by the Germans.

Now I'm not predicting, but if one wants to predict, if one wants to focus one's mind, does one think there will be increasing resistance of this kind, bearing in mind that the whole Maastricht process was a case of the enlightened, liberal, middle group of the Community – the élite – wanting something that the general public either was not enthusiastic about or, if asked, actually would be opposed to it. But of course that may change. In Britain, I can't conceive of any situation that Britain will join. In Italy, I think there is a desire, but whether there is the ability to make that commitment, I don't know.

May I just say one more thing? All this convergence idea – that you have to get to similar rates of inflation – there's something illogical about that. Once you have monetary union, presumably expectations should adjust completely. And the whole object of the monetary union is to have identical inflation rates, so why is it necessary to converge the inflation rates? I mean, once it's announced that on January 1 there will be a new money and that somebody else will control the money supply, well then, presumably, from that day onward inflation rates will converge. And crucially, wages and the labor market should adjust. Of course if you say that people are very irrational, that they can't accept this, then there is a problem.

Samuelson: Could I just speak to that last point? The colossal error made in 1925 by a reluctant Chancellor of the Exchequer, Winston Churchill (egged on in his reluctance by Keynes), to put the pound back at the pre-World War I level was misguided by exactly that consideration. First, by the trivial form of purchasing-power parity – the law of one price in one market for easily tradable goods. The wholesale-price indexes had already adjusted to what was expected to be the decision of the Chancellor. So people said, 'What's to worry about? We're already there'. But they weren't already there in an equilibrium steady-state sense; they were there in a way that would cause a great deal of trouble because it wasn't an equilibrium state. Yours, Max, is a variant. Your argument is: well, if they're not already there, they're damned well going to have to be there because that's what the rules of the game are. Well, it's damned well having to accommodate to the rules of the game, if the system has not spontaneously already contrived itself into a near situation, that is precisely what causes blood in the streets and changes in unemployment rates and turnovers of conservative parties in Canada, and so forth. So I think it would be extremely desirable if you're going to start passing batons, to try to pass them between two persons who are running at about the same speed, rather than to say: the law is that the baton must pass regardless of their speeds; it must happen.

Corden: Basically, I agree with you. What you have to have is a high degree of wage flexibility to make the system work, and my conclusion from all this is that that's one of the main problems about the whole business.

Sven W. Arndt: I think Max is right. The answer to Frankel's question – where do these fiscal criteria come from? – is simple: the Bundesbank wanted to make the whole process as difficult as possible, to delay the events of Maastricht as long as possible, and that was one way to do it. You've got those criteria from the central bankers – in particular, from the Bundesbank.

But I want to raise another question, an issue Jim Tobin spoke about. Why all this emphasis on convergence? We don't worry about convergency in the United States all that much. I think the reason you want convergence before you take the next step is because you don't think you've got a system that can deal with diversity. I think that's been the problem in Europe all along; the Europeans aren't sure that they're building a system that can tolerate diversity.

Christopher mentioned briefly – he didn't elaborate – convergence in the labor market. I'm not clear what that means. I can make sense of it if it means that the Europeans don't think they have the mobility, either within countries or between countries, to use labor markets for adjustment purposes. So they need convergence. But if convergence is what they want, then Christopher does need to worry about convergence in dealing with shocks. And he's not going to get that. That's one thing Europe can't legislate for or introduce within the Community. And they are going to have shocks. I agree with the earthquake analogy; you can't predict them, but you're going to get them. Several of us live in California; we can't predict earthquakes, but we try to do things to get ready for them, to adjust for them. And it's not clear to me that Europe is doing that.

I think Maastricht is dead, but there will be other versions of Maastricht. The Europeans feel they must keep moving ahead. They'll do something, they'll fake it; it won't be the Maastricht that's written down in the treaty of the Maastricht that most of us have in mind, but it's going to be something that's called Maastricht. However, that won't get away from this basic problem of how Europe then deals with diversity and with shocks.

Mundell: I've often been puzzled by the difference in views across the Atlantic – particularly between American economists and European economists. American economists are typically opposed to EMU, and they make up all kinds of reasons for that. One can think of explanations for this. A lot of Americans may look askance at the idea of a big powerful European government or European currency. But I think there's another explanation. It's something that comes from the different perspectives of people in the United States and all other countries. When there's an asymmetry between big and little countries, the bigger the big country, the more unconvincing it is for that country to think in terms of a fixed exchange-rate system. What currency would the United States peg the dollar to? All other currencies are much smaller transactions areas. But when you're a small country, then it's very easy to choose the country to which you would want to peg your currency.

Look, for example, at the fixed exchange-rate system that's existed asymmetrically between Austria and Germany. The Austrian schilling and the D-Mark have been fixed for many years, so Austria gets the same low rate of inflation that Germany has. And there's very little speculation about a change in that rate. The same is true, a little bit less so, with the Dutch guilder; it's quite clear what currency area the Dutch are in. Small countries – Belgium, Holland, Denmark, Austria – find it very natural to gravitate toward the D-Mark currency area.

For other countries, the picture may be different. The bigger the country, the more scope for independence. If you look at Italy, I think most Italians would say, yes, we would have a much better monetary policy if we had a fixed exchange-rate system that really works. If you look at England – I don't know whether the British would agree with me – I certainly think that if England had had a fixed exchange rate with the dollar, they would have had a much better inflation record, and they would probably have had a much more stable economy. France has its own special problems, but has actually had what amounts to almost a fixed exchange rate with the dollar; the French franc now is about the same as it was in the 1960s. That's partly a reflection of the nature of the French economy, with its big agricultural sector. It's more similar to the US economy than the manufacturing countries are.

Now, with respect to shocks in the system, there was a unification shock in Germany resulting in a big budget deficit that was financed to a large extent by the outside world. Germany had a $57 billion current-account surplus in 1989, and by 1992 it had a $25 billion deficit. So over that period there was a more than $80 billion turnaround – an enormous shock for Germany. And the ERM broke up, essentially, as a result of that shock because Germany, as part of the adjustment process, had to tighten its monetary policy, and that attracted the capital which financed the unification. That was a short-run situation, but it broke up the ERM. First Italy and Spain, then Britain got out of it. I agree with what was said yesterday about speculators, who did Britain a great favor by forcing it out of a system that it should never have joined at the greatly overvalued exchange rate with which it went in. The mistake of Britain was like its mistake in 1925 of getting into a fixed exchange-rate mechanism at a very much overvalued rate.

But suppose there had been a European currency at the time of German unification. Then I believe that the system would have worked very well. Imagine that you had a common European money for twelve countries, a single central bank, and a monetary policy that was increasing the money supply at a rate designed to preserve general price stability. I think the adjustment process would have worked out quite smoothly. Under any monetary system, you're not going to escape the real aspects of such a shock, but the unification shock would have accounted for only a small proportion of the Community-wide GDP, and I think could have been weathered. It would have been like a big shock in California or a big shock in Texas or in New England – something like that. I think the adjustment process would have worked out quite smoothly.

The one argument against monetary union that many people make is that it throws away the devaluation weapon. That argument of course can be applied to the United States, which is a big monetary union. When the United States was hit by the big oil shocks of the 1970s, New England had a big deficit, and if New England had had a separate currency, it could, and probably would, have devalued. Then, when the shocks were reversed in 1985 with the fall in the price of oil, Texas became a basket case, and if Texas had had a separate currency, it probably would have let the currency depreciate. And in the short run, that might have been better for the Texans. However, in the long run, we would have had a fragmented currency system; we would have had all those destabilizing expectations, and we would have been without the great advantages – the bonus of the common American currency area. That bonus will exist to a very large extent for the Europeans once they enter a monetary union.

My arguments for a European monetary union are like my arguments for fixed exchange rates for the world economy. I think the world economy is much better served by a system like the gold standard or like the Bretton Woods system, because the thing that characterized the Bretton Woods period, and even more the gold standard, was that you had not only a high degree of monetary discipline but also a high degree of fiscal discipline if the system was going to work.

Now my argument for European monetary union isn't only economic. I think on economic grounds there are pluses and minuses, and on balance the pluses outweigh the minuses. But the political arguments for it to me are overwhelming, and these have increased since German unification. You've got now a big country, a quasi-superpower, a potential real superpower – a very strong Germany in Europe, coupled with a power vacuum in Eastern Europe and an unstable arrangement in the former Soviet Union. I agree with Christopher that if Germany wants to move ahead toward monetary union, it would be crazy for the other European countries not to lock Germany into it, because I think that would lead to a much more stable European continent. This would be a healthy thing for the world, and I think that the political advantages for the United Stages of a European currency would outweigh any economic disadvantages that the US might encounter from a new form of competition.

Wakatsuki: I recall that Hans Tietmeyer, now the president of the Bundesbank, mentioned that there are two movements in European union. One is the movement of 'deepening' and the other is the movement of 'widening'. Deepening refers to economic convergence and increased cooperation in common defense policies, social policies, and so on, and this process of deepening perhaps may be the more important. Widening refers to geographical expansion – increasing membership. Sweden, Norway and other countries are already applying for membership.* These processes of deepening and widening could be mutually inconsistent, because inevitably the effort of deepening would be made more difficult by the enlargement of membership. Unless Europe goes to a two-speed arrangement, it might be wise to pay more attention to the matter of widening. It would be more difficult to have a twelve-country convergence, including Greece and Portugal, than to have Sweden or Austria in a deepening process.

Another point I'd like to raise is the impact of this currency unification on the world exchange market. The single currency in Europe – does that mean more stability in the world exchange market and in the world economy as a whole? The answer could be that it doesn't automatically guarantee any stability. That depends on the behavior of perhaps three major currencies. But at least historically, it's possible to think that if the European Monetary Union aims at price stability, that might mean more stability for the world economy at large. Another question, out of curiosity, what would be the impact on reserves and world trade if the European currencies are unified? Perhaps world reserves would shrink, because quite a large portion of reserves held, say, in French francs or in Deutsche Marks would perhaps no longer be foreign reserves. At the same time, international trade within Europe would no longer be defined as international trade. But these effects on world monetary reserves and on world trade are mainly a matter of curiosity.

Cooper: Like Jeff Frankel, I feel a little awkward as an outsider commenting on an issue of such intense debate and feeling as the Maastricht Treaty. One of the great disappointments to me in this debate was the apparent inability of Europeans in that debate to separate the objective of European monetary union from the Maastricht Treaty. Either you were for the treaty

---

*Austria, Finland and Sweden Joined the European Union on January 1, 1995: Norway voted not to.

or you were against it, and if you were for the EMU you had to
be in favor of the treaty. If you were against the treaty, *ipso facto*
you were labeled as being against the EMU.

I'm in the awkward position of being in favor of European
monetary union – I have been for over twenty years – and being
very strongly against the Maastricht Treaty. I think the treaty is
preposterous. Christopher made the analogy this morning between the treaty and the Constitution of the United States. It is
there, it is embodied in stone, and it's now the basis on which the
Europeans will go forward. But I would just remind him that
before we had the Constitution we had the Articles of Confederation, and they proved in seven short years to be completely
unworkable. It was that experience that drove us to a more sensi-
ble document, which is the Constitution. I'd put the Maastricht
Treaty in the category of the Articles of Confederation.

We talked this morning a lot about the convergence criteria.
But there's another dimension which Paul Samuelson opened the
debate on yesterday that I'd like to drive home, and that is the
notion of central bank independence. This is not a self-defining
term. There is in fact a whole spectrum of independences, and a
distinction that I think is necessary but which the Europeans fail
to make is between central bank independence of the sitting
government – a criterion which the Federal Reserve meets, the
Bundesbank meets, the Swiss National Bank meets, and, in a
curious halfway, the Dutch central bank meets – and central bank
independence of the political process.

None of these central banks is independent of the political
process, and I believe that's a decisively important attribute of
any democratic society. All of them are created by simple statute,
and they can be changed by simple statute. Speaking especially
from the perspective of the Federal Reserve, but I know it's also
true to some extent in Germany, the central bankers are conscious of that fact, and the fact that their basic law – the Federal
Reserve Act or the basic law of the Bundesbank – can be changed
by statute puts limits on how far the central bankers are willing to
deviate from the drift of public opinion. It is not the formal
structure of the law that protects the Bundesbank; it's the high

reputation that it has with the German public. Any chancellor who wants to change the statute and has the votes – he can do that – would be putting his political life on the line. And that's exactly as it should be in a democratic society. Similarly, at any moment in time, there are lots of bills in the Congress aimed at changing the Federal Reserve Act. Most of them never go any place, most of them shouldn't go any place, a lot of them are completely preposterous. But they're there, and the Federal Reserve watches carefully congressional sentiment toward these various pieces of prospective legislation.

The Maastricht Treaty creates a body of platonic monetary guardians. They violate the first principle of democratic society, which is that people who make decisions that affect the public at large should be accountable to the public at large. They are accountable to no one. They are obliged to report once a year, but that's not the same as public accountability. They cannot be removed, they cannot be overridden. It's true that the ultimate recourse is to change the treaty. That could be done, but it's like a constitutional change in the United States. Moreover, it requires unanimity to change the treaty. So it seems to me that the Maastricht Treaty is flawed on fundamental grounds of democratic theory, and I don't see how any serious democrat in Europe – democrat with a small 'd' – can support the treaty. It widens an already wide democratic gap, as it's called in Europe, and for that reason as well as some of the more analytical points that have been touched on this morning, I believe that the Maastricht Treaty will not, and should not, go into effect in its current form. So I think outsiders can actually have played a potentially constructive role.

My next observation concerns the fiscal situation in the United States and what one might call the fiscal solidarity of the federal system, with a large federal budget toward each of the regions. The point I want to make – and this draws on research done by others, not by me – is that there is much less here than meets the eye. It is true that we have large interregional transfers within the United States – to southern California, for example, for defense spending, or to West Virginia as part of an Appalachian program.

But this is not disturbance-sensitive federal spending. It's worth mentioning that the Europeans also have large interregional transfers, partly through the common agricultural policy and partly through the social fund. Our transfers are not, for the most part, cyclically sensitive. It is true that when a region goes into a slump, as Texas did in the mid-1980s, it gets a lot of cushioning through the federal tax system, because taxes are very cyclically sensitive to changes in income. But that's true of any modern fiscal system. The cushioning effect comes from the fiscal system as such, not from the interregional aspect.

We do have a few components that are cyclically sensitive interregional transfers. Unemployment, remember, is state-financed in this country unless it's deemed to be longer term, meaning over 26 weeks, when federal support comes in, as it has done in the latest recession. So we have a few components of that, but they do not bulk large in the fiscal system. An important difference between the US and Europe is that when the federal government has to borrow more because income-tax revenue from Texas has gone down, the debt service is covered by the entire American population, whereas if the Dutch government has to borrow because Dutch revenues have gone down, the future fiscal burden is borne by the Dutch population in the absence of a European-wide fiscal system. That is an important difference, but in its economic effects it is second-order to the fact of being able to borrow in a European-wide and international capital market that the Europeans would have under a monetary union.

My final observation is that I long thought that by far the easiest way to achieve European monetary union would be to Europeanize an existing currency, and my candidate twenty years ago was the pound sterling, largely because of the talents, institutions, and so forth of London as a capital market and financial center. But the pound does not seem like a likely candidate these days. The only serious candidate, I think, would be the German mark, and if the Europeans are genuinely interested in a currency union as distinguished from a demonstrable public we've-gone-yet-another-step, what they would do is to allow the mark to circulate freely in all countries and actually become legal tender in parallel with the national currencies. That has some complications, but these are not insuperable, and when the extent of use of the mark in, let us say, the Netherlands reaches a certain point, the Dutch get a vote on the Bundesbank Council, or when it reaches that point in France, the French get a vote of three or four or five on the Bundesbank Council. Gradually over time, you enlarge the Bundesbank Council so that it becomes, not a German Council, but a European Council. This is a quixotic observation, because I don't see any political prospects of achieving what I've described. But the fact that there are no political prospects of doing it that way – which I think would be far and away the most straightforward and easiest way to achieve a European currency – should at least raise some of the questions that Max Corden and Jeffrey Frankel raised about the political will that actually lies behind these stated desires to achieve monetary union.

Frankel: This morning, I mentioned one possible theory as to why the fiscal criteria were there in Maastricht – namely, as an arbitrary but nevertheless perhaps useful test of political will. My analogy from Greek mythology is Theseus having to lift the stone. Max Corden and Sven Arndt both mentioned another on the list of possible explanations of why the fiscal criteria are there – namely, they're very difficult, almost impossible, and that was the point to make without saying no. The Bundesbank, in particular, was not enthusiastic about monetary union, and wanted to make it impossible. So I'm going to offer another analogy. There are actually two possibilities from mythology. First, when Jason went off for the Golden Fleece, it was supposed to be an impossible mission; that was the point of the whole thing. It was a way of getting rid of him so he would never come back to claim his kingdom. Another example – this from American mythology – is the Wizard of Oz. When the wizard sent Dorothy off for the broom of the wicked Witch of the West, that was supposed to be an impossible mission. In both cases, the mission was accomplished, but this is mythology, after all.

I promised Dick I'd try to move the discussion a little bit eastward. One more possible analogy that might be fitting comes from eastern tradition rather than western mythology, in which the hero is always supposed to accomplish something. I'm thinking of the Buddhist or Hindu principle of self-abnegation and the willpower not to do anything. If you're meditating and a fly lands on your nose, you have the willpower not to scratch it. I think this is perhaps the most fitting analogy on what is necessary for a European country not to do. When a European country suffers a downturn in demand, it should have the willpower to refrain from scratching it; otherwise, it should not give up its independent currency.

On the prospects for passing some of these tests, Bob Mundell gave us two historical episodes which illustrate the difficulty of maintaining a common currency or a fixed exchange rate if you start at an overvalued level. In a sense, that's tragic in that it's avoidable. The two examples that Bob mentioned were the UK in 1925 going back on the gold standard and the UK again in 1990 entering the exchange-rate mechanism – in both cases at too high a parity. I would like to add a third recent historical episode to this list in the interest of moving the discussion eastward a little more seriously. German monetary union, I think, was a real tragedy. This is a rare case where economic textbooks had the right answer, which was that the East Germans were less productive than West Germans by a magnitude of 2 or 3, and that if you're going to unify the two currencies – and there are very good arguments for it – it should have been done at an exchange rate of 2 to 1 or 3 to 1. I think if that had been done, a lot of the problems that Germany is facing today would have been much reduced.

Where a country already is a member of a currency union and there's a long historical record of a fixed exchange rate, things are easier. It's only new shocks that you have to worry about, and it's more likely that you can withstand them. In this connection, the Benelux countries come up from time to time and the French-speaking African countries. Both currency areas are for the first time under threat, and these are the last regions in the world that seemed to have some degree of truly credible commitment to rigidly fixed exchange rates. In the last twenty years, we have seen progressively more and more of the exchange rates that seemed fixed give way. In the early 1970s, many of the former British colonies remained pegged to the pound sterling, and most of the Latin American countries remained pegged to the dollar. Well, all those links have been severed by now. The French African countries remained pegged to the French franc – almost the last example in the world of exchange rates that seemed really fixed – yet this month [January 1994] they finally decided to devalue against the French franc. Similarly, Benelux, which I would have thought is the best example of an irrevocably fixed currency union, ...

Johnson: [interrupting]   You mean Belgium–Luxembourg; you don't mean the Netherlands.

Frankel: Well, I mean all three.

Johnson: Benelux is not a currency union.

Frankel: Not a currency union, but an arrangement that was credible and was going to stick. The problem is that to the extent that there is a fissure between the French franc and the German mark, Belgium is more likely to go the way of – might go the way of – the French franc and the Netherlands go the way of the Deutsche Mark. And Luxembourg is the one that is torn. I would have thought that Luxembourg was the best example, out of all the countries in the world, of a very small, very open country that of course is going to maintain its fixed peg, and yet even that is under question because the country is being torn in these two directions.

Moving eastward, one has to think of the regions that have broken up. Czechoslovakia had a common currency, the Soviet Union had a common currency, yet both cases ended in a split. This is, I think, a warning against the view that what it takes is will-power; forget Stage One and Stage Two, and let's jump directly to Stage Three, because if we just go ahead and do it, it will be irrevocable. But nothing here is truly irrevocable, and if the political pressures get bad enough, you will eventually have to break up. So that's a reason to think carefully before you do it.

Solomon: I have a question on the German unification issue. Jeff, you say that if currency conversion had been done on a 2 to

1 or 3 to 1 basis, it would have made a big difference. I'm not clear on this. On unification, the Deutsche Mark became the currency of the whole country. Now what does 2 to 1, 3 to 1 mean? It means that East Germans would have less purchasing power than if you had done that at the exchange rates you mentioned rather than 1 to 1. But how much difference would that have made to the basic problem, which I take to be the fact that productivity in East Germany was some fraction of what it was in West Germany? Once unification occurred, there was an enormous motivation for wages in East Germany to move upward toward the West German level, and that's what's creating great difficulties for East German industry. Would any of that have been influenced by a different exchange rate?

Cooper: Max, are you on the same point?

Corden: Yes, exactly this point. I raise a very simple question: does a monetary union, like that between East and West Germany, encourage a tendency to wage equalization or trade-union integration? If it does, then we can say that the monetary union did help to cause this bad effect. If it doesn't, then it wouldn't have mattered what the exchange rate was.

Tobin: That's the question.

Frankel: I should clarify what I'm saying they should have done. In the early stages, every East German who made it to the west got 100 marks, or something like that. I think they should have been given 10,000 marks or very generous terms, but should have been told, 'Welcome to the west, we love you, but this is the last thing you're getting from us. From now on, your wages will be what they were, but converted into Deutsche Marks at 2 to 1'.

One really cannot separate the exchange-rate policy from wage policy. The point is that it's very hard for someone who's lived under the other system to make the mental adjustment to the western system, which is that if you want to attain western standards of living and get all these wonderful consumer goods, you're going to have to earn them. The West Germans, and Chancellor Kohl in particular, lost a very valuable opportunity to send the right signal. The right signal should have been: if you want to attain West German living standards, you're going to have to attain West German productivity standards. And that signal should have been sent in part through the terms on which the exchange rate was fixed and in part through wage policy also. The signal they sent was exactly the opposite – that the way to attain West German living standards is to vote for our political party and to join our unions and to go forth through this political and union process. I think it's going to take many years to unlearn that lesson.

Arndt: Jeff, I thought one of the reasons Germans give for speeding up equalization of wages had to do with the tendency of East Germans to migrate west. That created problems – pressures on the housing stock and on infrastructure in general, so the argument was: let's eliminate the incentive for migration by narrowing the wage gap.

Frankel: Yes, I think that's right, but there's the question: what is the most powerful incentive to migration, unemployment or wage differentials? And I think the answer is unemployment. A survey in Germany provided strong evidence that this was the case – that people who were moving or considering moving were doing it, not because there was a wage differential but because they had lost their jobs in the east or were worried about losing their jobs. And the point, of course, is that as long as the productivity level is different – and in the best possible scenario, it would have to take years for the differential to disappear – nobody in his right mind is likely to invest in the east as long as unit labor costs are much higher than in the west. Therefore, jobs are not created, and therefore the migration to the west.

Cooper: That's my view, not only in retrospect, but at the time. That was the genuine problem, to which the alleged solution was in fact not a solution at all. All you have to do is think it through. The Germans were making a gamble which had about two chances in a hundred of being right – that East Germany was just like West Germany, once they took away the control system and put in market-oriented things, and that therefore East German productivity could be expected to rise in a couple of years to West German levels with a little bit of western management, access to western markets, and so on. Well, one could not have ruled that out a priori, but it was an extremely improbable event. That was the gamble that was taken. The German labor unions targeted wage parity by 1994, and the German government officially accepted that. That's now been pushed off to 1996, but it has not been abandoned as a target at all. My guess is that the target will be postponed again and yet again and yet again. In the meantime, wages have risen about twice as fast as productivity has risen in eastern Germany.

Solomon: There is not much the exchange rate would have done about those basic problems.

Cooper: I thought Jeff made the point that the exchange rate here is a surrogate for something quite different, which is what East German wages should have been, measured in D-Marks. That's not, strictly speaking, an exchange-rate question.

Tobin: But at the beginning what should the exchange rate have been? There's nothing to stop wages from rising.

Cooper: Afterward, no – particularly as productivity rises.

Tobin: Well, even if it doesn't.

Cooper: For whatever reasons.

Frankel: I think this is the kind of question for which textbook economics gave you the right answer. Now when I say that, some economists say, 'Look, it doesn't matter; textbooks say that wages adjust, costs give way, the exchange rate is irrelevant'. Well, it depends on which textbook you use [laughter]. But I think the point about sending the signal is very important, and exchange-rate policy was part of it. My preferred policy would have been explicitly to say, 'I'm sorry, this parity is not going to work; your initial wages are going to be determined by what they have been, converted at an exchange rate of 2 to 1'.

Mundell: I think much of what Jeff said is correct. I agree with it on economic grounds, but I think that the German government was faced with political decisions, and it had to do something that was going to be palatable. Everything had to be done quickly, because at that time there were people who were worried that the Soviet Union might take back its permission for German unification. Things were done quickly, and I think on balance they were done as well as any country could have. What's remarkable about this is that Germany has done this without running a big current-account deficit. Germany can easily afford this investment in eastern Germany, and its budget deficit in relation to GDP is still the lowest of any country in the Economic Community with the exception of Ireland.

Cooper: If you don't count the off-budget items. But if you count public-sector borrowing requirements, that's not true. If you exclude the off-budget items, that's like excluding the US savings-and-loan bailout – taking that out of the US budget.

Mundell: Right, but those items are excluded for all the other countries too, aren't they?

Johnson: When the IMF does the figures, yes.

Mundell: So, if you include the off-budget items, the German budget deficit is not 3.8 percent of GDP; let's say it's 5 percent or 6 percent. But, compared to the other countries of Europe, that seems to me to be par for the course – not worse. And over this period, Germany has maintained a high degree of stability. The mark is still strong, and I think that in view of the seriousness of the shock, the performance of the German economy would have to be rated maybe as a B rather than as a C or a C–.

Now I want to pick up on Dick's comment about European monetary union. I too have had the belief in the 1960s and early 1970s that the easiest way to create a European currency union was to use an existing currency, and in my paper, 'A Plan for a European Currency' in 1970 that I presented at a conference in Madrid and also to the European Economic Community Commission, I did suggest that the pound sterling was an appropriate currency for that purpose. Now in the 1970s it became clear that the mark would be a better candidate. If would be quite an easy matter technically to use the mark as the European currency. You could have a European board in Frankfurt, so you wouldn't even have to change buildings, just change the people. The Bundesbank could buy up all the European currencies and replace them with marks, and you could have an instant European currency. You could start with a stamp on them saying this is an ecu, or a certain number of these is equal to an ecu, and then you could reprint them with new symbols on. Instead of Konrad Adenauer, you could put Michelangelo, as the Italians do, or Shakespeare, or something like that.

You could go this way, and it would be the way of getting most quickly to currency union. I made this proposal last year at a meeting in Lyon at the Ecu Institute. Lyon is one of the cities that had hoped to be a center of the monetary community, and a French representative at that meeting convinced me that the rest of Europe would never accept a mark-centered currency. Certainly France would never accept that proposal, and I think that people in Britain would take the attitude that if Germany is going to be part of the operation, then it must make concessions like all the other countries.

I think that this is the reason why that kind of proposal would not be accepted. In fact, the process of getting to European monetary union is almost as important as the reality of actually being there. Since the Common Market was created, the process of European unification has been the best game that's been going on in Europe, the most exciting thing for the European people, and maybe it doesn't matter if they get to union by 1997 or 1999. It may be 2010, but the process of working toward it gives Europe a sense of purpose that it's never had before, and I believe that the Europeans will have to go through it in this slow way.

Now I made the comment at our meeting here three years ago that time was running out on the Community and that the Community really had to move quickly because of Germany. I thought that maybe after Germany had absorbed the eastern part, it would like its independence and its greater mark area much more than it would like European political union, which would be one of the tendencies toward which monetary union would lead. I'm still not sure whether that's true; I hope I was wrong on that. Maybe time isn't that important. Maybe Germany will still think that association with the rest of Europe will be a favorable thing.

While I don't think any longer that European countries would use the mark as a European currency, I do think that something close to that may occur. European monetary union certainly is going to be at least a multi-stage process; it won't be an all-at-once process. Greece is going to have a hard time joining a monetary union in any reasonable time, and Italy may be slow, but I think that it would be feasible to start off with a small core of countries that are ready to join. Maybe if you got Germany, the Benelux countries and France (and Britain now that it's changed its exchange rate); once things got started in that framework, it would be much easier for other countries to come in. Even though you wouldn't use the Deutsche Mark, that will be the currency around which the other currencies will have to strike their exchange rates. The mark will be the the de facto numeraire for a while of the system, and the ecu will be related to that. I think the multi-stage process – first a core of countries – is still feasible in this century.

Tobin: I have a question for Dick on an earlier point, which was in relation to the treatment of budgetary outlays for temporary purposes, such as the savings-and-loan débâcle in the United States. If the purpose of the budget requirement is somehow to be a predictor of what the budget situation will be in the future when the monetary union occurs, then perhaps it's proper to omit the transitory deficits that are occurring for special purposes. In the United States, the costs of the savings-and-loan crisis in some sense should not have been included in the deficits of the years in which the outlays were being made but rather put back into the national debt that happened somewhat earlier, when the contingent liability suddenly became an actual liability. So I don't think your debate with Bob Mundell about how such expenditures were handled in Germany is really very relevant to what deficit you ought to think about.

Cooper: I agree with the thought behind that but, by the same token, then government sales of assets should be excluded from the budget.

Tobin: Of course, of course.

Cooper: But you can bet your life they're not going to do that [loud laughter].

Tobin: There are at least three advocates of monetary union here: Bob Mundell, Dick Cooper and Christopher Johnson. I would like to ask them the following question: by how much do you think the annual growth rate of the gross European product will be between, let's say, the year 2000 and the year 2030 if there is monetary union, compared with the situation in which the European Community otherwise exists without a common currency?

Cooper: Bob, do you want to take a stab at that?

Mundell: I'd say about three-quarters of 1 percent.

Tobin: Three-quarters of a percent per year?

Mundell: Per annum. And the major factor figuring into it is that in the absence of something like this, I would expect a European war.

Tobin: Okay, you don't have to explain that.

Cooper: Christopher, do you want to answer Jim's question? He has a very concrete, specific question.

Johnson: Yes, well, the gains quoted by the EC Commission, simply from the savings in transaction costs by having a single currency, were of the order of a quarter of 1 percent of GDP. However, there are much bigger dynamic gains due to having lower interest rates, which I think would bring us up to Bob's figure of three-quarters of 1 percent.

Cooper: If I may say so, I think that's greatly exaggerated, but I had not allowed for the contingency of war. I would guess 0.2 to 0.3 percent. I believe most European industry is organized oligopolistically, and I believe that to get the full competitive pressures of one market, you're actually going to need a single currency. But that doesn't translate into big changes in the growth rate, so I would say that over a 30-year period, maybe 0.2 of 1 percent would be my rough answer to Jim's question.

Solomon: Dick, do you want to explain how it is that a single currency eliminates oligopoly in a way that the complete removal of trade barriers and the opening of markets that has already occurred do not do?

Cooper: You open up a complex issue, and you don't want a lecture from me on this question, but the presence of different currency areas gives oligopolies an occasion, a mutually recognized occasion, for keeping markets separate and insulating one another from competition that would otherwise take place. Some of it is actually true official action, and some of it comes through corporate behavior, which has to do with hedging currency risks. Both of these developments are at the expense of consumers. It remains to be seen how competition policy develops within Europe.

Mundell: Jim, how much do you think the rate of growth of GDP in the United States would be affected by splitting up the US monetary system into the twelve Federal Reserve Districts, each with a separate central bank and with flexible exchange rates between them? How much would growth rates be affected between now and, say, 2030?

Tobin: I'm not in favor of doing that. I think it would reduce the growth rate of the American economy, let's say, by 0.2 percent per annum, but that doesn't really answer the question, because departing from the present arrangements would be a costly thing to do in itself. On the question raised by Bob Solomon, I would have thought that almost all of the competitive gains that Cooper referred to could be achieved with separate currencies, just by having a completely free-trade area.

Cooper: Let me mention one thing that I didn't mention in response to Bob Solomon, and that is that profit margins on manufactured goods are not terribly high – 5 percent on average; for Fortune 500, I think, it's $6^{1}/_{2}$ percent in a non-recession year. The kinds of currency movements that we see are driven, not by what economists like to call fundamentals, but by relatively short-term financial market phenomena. An overwhelming number of transactions are purely financial transactions, not purchases of goods and services. When exchange rates move, a manufacturer can find his entire profit wiped out for reasons totally beyond his ken because of something going on in Frankfurt or New York or London. Now he can hedge – not without cost – a particular transaction, but what he can't do is hedge on investment. Total investment will therefore be less than it would be if there were no exchange risk. So I see some long-term efficiency advantages associated with a currency union.

To change the subject, I think we ought to give Christopher Johnson a chance to respond to a number of mostly not very friendly – well-meaning but not very friendly – comments about

Maastricht. Christopher, would you address the question which has come up now a few times: how do you see the Maastricht process fitting in with the enlargement process? We now have four countries that hope to become full members of the Community by 1995, we have four more that are just waiting to put their applications in as soon as they get a signal, and then three to five countries behind them. Just one factual thing: I don't know the answer to the question whether if Sweden, for example, joins the Community in 1995, does Sweden automatically sign on to Maastricht by virtue of its Community membership or, as was discussed at one time, is that a separate process?

Johnson:　Well, I don't know the answer to your legal question, but I may have more allies around the table than I thought, because when I heard Jeff Frankel listing the conditions for an optimum currency area, I ticked them off one by one, and I thought we are quite close to fulfilling these conditions as a result of the economic integration we've already had. But I would add that by entering a monetary union we do make it more likely that these conditions for an optimum currency area will be fulfilled to an even greater extent. In other words, many of the conditions of a successful monetary union can only be realized by setting one up and then allowing various processes to take place which will not in fact operate fully until people know that they're in a currency union.

Paul Samuelson made a point about the high cost of intervention. His criticism was very much the standard one that was being made by a number of people who were saying that the exchange-rate mechanism – the ERM – was a very unstable way of getting to monetary union. But the point I would make is that by now having 15 percent dams on exchange rates, we have in fact sidestepped the frontal assault of the speculators. Currencies have on the whole behaved rather stably without the necessity to intervene, and it's a moot point to what extent one will need to narrow the bands before entering full monetary union. Once we have entered it, the kind of fixed exchange rates we would have to have until we can print enough bank notes and change computer systems are quite different from the Bretton Woods type of fixed exchange rates, because national currencies will then just become manifestations of the European currency until we can actually get the single currency. But Paul wants to say something.

Samuelson: I wish I thought that yours was a satisfactory answer to my query and my concern, but I think that when, under narrow bands, the system is developing earthquake strains, under a wider band that would show itself in certain regions being at the lower end of the band. And at the lower end of the band, there is reconstructed all the reasons for my concern and all the reasons for the delight of speculators.

Johnson: I absolutely recognize your point. It's too early to test the 15 percent system fully. I suspect that when currencies get into the lower part of the band and stay there, there will be a case for realigning them so they can use the full freedom of the 15 percent again. This was the topic of a seminar paper I gave at the IMF which I am developing into a working paper – how we can somehow have stability, not so much of nominal as of real exchange rates, so that currencies which temporarily have higher inflation will adjust their exchange rates within these bands, but those which have similar convergent low inflation rates, and are sound on fundamentals, may be able to stay close together in nominal exchange-rate terms, which will be more or less the same in real exchange-rate terms. This is a good way of satisfying the test that countries should be able to compete with each other. Once they're in a monetary union, they won't be able to change nominal exchange rates, so it would be well to make sure that they go in at a proper set of real exchange rates.

In answer to Max Corden, I would say that we shouldn't write off the possibility of Britain joining the monetary union. We have a Chancellor of the Exchequer, Kenneth Clarke, who is a closet European; he doesn't want to alienate the right-wing opponents in his party by saying it openly. He may well be prime minister before the next election and then declare his hand as a good European before an election in 1996, just in time for the first Maastricht deadline. However, if the present government loses the next election, there will then be a Labour Party or Labour–

Liberal coalition government, which is much more likely to take Britain into Europe than a Conservative government led by John Major or even by Kenneth Clarke. So I think the answer is, wait until after the next election and you may get a surprise.

Bob Mundell said quite rightly that the US hardly needs to be persuaded about the advantages of a single currency, as it has had one which served it well for over two centuries. So we're really saying, not why can't a woman be more like a man, but just why can't Europe be more like the United States in this respect, without necessarily setting up a centralized federal government? Bob also criticized the UK for coming in at too high an exchange rate when it joined the ERM. It could have solved this problem by devaluing; unfortunately, it wanted the French to devalue as well, and they wouldn't. There was a certain amount of macho rivalry to see whether the pound or the franc was the stronger currency. The ideal would have been a revaluation of the D-Mark against all other currencies, which unfortunately was not possible.

I naturally have a great deal of sympathy with Dick Cooper's observations, but I would just point out that the Maastricht Treaty has already gone into operation. We are in Stage Two; I think it would be very difficult at this stage to repeal the treaty. I think the best thing to do is to interpret it. On another point, Dick claimed that the European central bank would not be accountable. But of course the Bundesbank isn't accountable to anybody either. In that respect, it's not the best model, and I think by making the European central bank report to the European Parliament and to the Council, you are creating what most people would call accountability. The European central bank doesn't have to ask anybody before it does something, but it sure as hell has to explain afterwards why it did it, which is perhaps a little bit like the relationship between the Fed and the president and Congress.

Then there was the point which both Bob Mundell and Dick Cooper made about using the D-Mark as the single currency. As Bob says, it's politically unacceptable to the French, because many of us hope that a European central bank would not have quite such a tough monetary policy as the Bundesbank – that it would pay more attention to unemployment, economic growth, and other objectives, as the Fed does. Of course that is precisely why the Germans, and the Bundesbank in particular, are not very keen to exchange the Bundesbank for a European central bank.

Now I'll just conclude on a question which Dick raised, and that is with respect to the enlargement of the existing European Community and the exchange-rate mechanism. On political grounds, I think that enlargement is highly desirable. The former Soviet countries are not yet ready for it, but there are four EFTA countries lining up, which are Austria, Norway, Sweden and Finland. The Scandinavian countries have problems over things like oil and fisheries and welfare, and only if these countries join or agree to join this year will they be in time to observe the convergence criteria for entry into a monetary union by 1996; 1998 would of course give them another two years. Except in the case of Austria, these four countries may not pass the convergence criteria, and we therefore have the possibility that we will have a narrow monetary union. Some countries would go in first, and the number of countries in the second tier would become much larger if it included Scandinavia as well as Portugal, Spain – even the United Kingdom. You would then have to have a new style of exchange-rate mechanism where these countries would peg their exchange rates to the new single currency, the ecu. All this is envisaged under the Maastricht Treaty, and it's anybody's guess how well it would work. My own preference is for getting everybody into the single currency at the same time if possible, and then we can think about further enlargement to include the former Soviet satellites, who have got much more to do in order to get their economies anywhere near convergent with even the weakest members of the existing twelve-member European Community.

8.   Problems in the Former Communist Countries

Introduced by Richard N. Cooper

Chairman Cooper: The agenda that we agreed to yesterday morning includes a discussion of former communist countries, and I don't know how much time we want to spend on those. Then there is the rest of the world. I've asked Bob Solomon to lead off the discussion on what we inappropriately call the Third World. After that, we want to spend a little time this afternoon on Bob Mundell's suggestions for the international monetary system as a whole, and he's going to introduce the discussion on that.

We could spend a lot of time discussing the enormous transformations in Eastern Europe and in the former Soviet Union. However, we don't have the time to spend a lot of time doing that, but at least I ought to open the subject for any observations that any of you would like to make. And perhaps by way of stimulating the discussion, I should observe that my colleague and sometime adviser to the Russian government, Jeffrey Sachs, has pelted the world's leadership in the *Los Angeles Times* a couple of days ago [January, 1994], in *The New Republic* and in *The New York Times* in a series of trenchant criticisms of the G–7 about the way they have treated Russia in particular, arguing that what we've seen since the fall of 1991 has been a unique historic opportunity. We should have seized it boldly and constructively, and in his judgement we've muffed it. He gives less than 50–50 probability of having another chance, but he says it can't be ruled out and that if we do have one more chance we should be prepared to exploit it. He takes the occasion in these various fusillades to blast the International Monetary Fund. I do not agree with him on that point. I think the IMF is being made a scapegoat for deficiencies by the G–7 in general and by the US in particular, although the US in this regard has lots of support from Japan and from European countries. Basically, we wanted to do something and not spend any money doing it in a situation that required a lot of money. We put the IMF out front, and it was predictably incapable of handling the job. With that as background, does anyone want to address this issue – particularly the monetary aspects?

Solomon: It's a nice question. Jim Tobin and I talked about it; we probably don't agree, and there may be disagreement around the table. What difference would it have made to Russia to have had more foreign exchange, more aid? This is what Jeff Sachs is complaining about, no doubt – quite apart from the conditionality of the IMF. What difference would it have made to Russian reformists if more financial aid had been made available to them? That, I think, is an important question, and I'm not sure of the answer to it.

Cooper: Let me try to put the Sachs case as I understand it – and as I understand it, I'm more likely to agree with it than with what may be his real argument. It is not that western aid can be in some fundamental sense decisive in a process which is necessarily a domestic dynamic that the Russian people have to work out for themselves. Nor is it a question of conditionality; he wants the aid to be not *carte blanche* but subject to heavy conditions. So his quarrel is with the details of conditions rather than with the principle of conditionality and the niggardliness of the aid.

Now what is the role of the aid in Sachs's view? It's essentially betting on a team whose political support in Russia is tenuous – to guard our team, giving it a chance to make the necessary reforms in a way that, if not politically popular, at least is not so unpalatable to the public as to make them reject the team like a bad virus. To make the team survive, in his view, required some visible sign of progress, and one way to do that would be to have a substantial amount of imports – generalized import support – conditioned on policy steps that the Russians would take. He rejects strongly the notion that shock therapy has failed in Russia. He says, and in this I agree with him, that shock therapy has not been tried. The Russians did some things quite dramatically in early 1992, but they did not take the full package of shock therapy, including in particular the fiscal package. And it's part of the Sachs program that he would provide budget support specifically for the creation of at least a primitive social safety net.

One of the problems in all centrally planned economies is that each person's life revolves around the enterprise for which he works. His children's education, his health care, his housing, his vacations – everything is linked to the firm, so the firm is not merely an economic entity; it's a quasi-governmental entity as well. And for a market economy to work, the economic functions of enterprises have to be separated from their social role. Sachs argues that the G–7 and the western world should have pushed the Russians harder in the direction of creating an independent labor market and an independent social safety net, because unemployment inevitably would be rising. You don't want to leave people in the lurch, and this is a constructive way in which you could have promoted reforms and spent the money doing it, which would have showed up through additional imports into the Russian system.

So that's the case as I understand it. And once the team loses credibility or political support in Russia, it's very unlikely to have a second chance.

Tobin: The need for dollars to balance the rouble budget is not really obvious. You say, well, the dollars will end up being bought by somebody, presumably the recipients of the budgetary expenditures, and used for imports. But in that scenario, there's no way in which you can be sure what the imports will be or to whom they will go.

Cooper: Correct.

Tobin: One thing that struck me about the things I've read by Jeffrey Sachs and other advisers to Russia is that if one looks at the Russian situation without attention to the monetary and financial aspects, one would say that the principal problem is the transfer of resources from their present activities to other activities – to activities that have social value, either to individuals or to the whole society, from those that now do not. That's a big shift; that's a big problem – moving resources around. And when I hear the big problem described as simply avoiding hyperinflation, and am not told how getting rid of hyperinflation will be sufficient to do the other job, the real job of shifting resources, then I wonder about what the strategy is.

I certainly don't think you should have hyperinflation, but you should have your eye on what the ultimate goal is. The ultimate goal is not to produce a lot of unemployment but to shift resources from where they are to something else. And I notice that in a situation that has some similarities to the situation after World War II in Europe, where the objective was to rebuild market economies – capitalistic economies – the people who had that goal in mind, like Jean Monnet, did not think you could do it simply by hoping that a market economy with new enterprises and all that would arise from the ashes without any planning by anybody – without any projects which would involve governmental guidance and cooperation along with the restoration of productive enterprises. But what you hear in Moscow and in the reading I did is that you can't do that in Russia because the government can't do anything right. There is a sort of faith on the part of the reformers that if you make these people unemployed, then their availability as workers will somehow result in there being a new sector of market enterprises that will employ them – a matter of extreme faith in the working of a market system that doesn't exist.

Cooper: I think there are two analytical points that are partially responsive to what you say. One is that, compared with western societies, all the communist countries had much too much manufacturing production and far too few services. So part of the shift in resources that you were alluding to would be from the manufacturing sector to services, where capital requirements are not zero, but low. It's largely a question of human organization. I think the tie-in with hyperinflation is that the main source of expenditure and printing of money is to provide continuing subsidies to enterprises that produce goods of low or no social value.

Tobin: I understand that. I don't approve of this policy at all, but just suppose that the central bank, in pursuing this terrible

monetary policy, had made loans not to the existing manufacturing enterprises and military contractors, which they have been
doing in order to pay people to do nothing or to produce things
that nobody wants, but instead had made loans to new entrepre-
neurs. The monetary effects would have been the same, but you'd
have the new enterprises. That's just a mental experiment to
point out that it may not be that the financial reform, which ought
to be made, is either necessary or sufficient to get a long move
forward on the main job.

Johnson: Well, I've visited Russia a couple of times in the
last two years, and the impression I have is that there are two
policy strands. One is financial stabilization, which is the kind of
thing the IMF deals with. The other is industrial restructuring,
which is a much more long-term thing which typically the World
Bank and other development institutions deal with. I think that
these two policies are in some sense separate. If you go too hard
on the financial stabilization, you may make industrial restructuring more difficult. In other words, there has to be some mechanism whereby you withdraw credit from terribly badly run firms,
but you maintain credit to ordinary Russian badly run firms. The
danger is that if you withdraw credit from every Russian enterprise, you will get a Schumpeterian process of creative destruc-
tion. Something, no doubt, will rise from the ashes, but a lot of
people will be unemployed, and you may get social and political
unrest which would be impossible for anybody to handle.

What seems to be happening is that, as Dick says, there's a
need to shift into services, and many people are becoming rich in
perhaps the wrong services – foreign-exchange dealing, with-
holding supplies to maintain prices, and so on. So people are
getting rich, but they're the wrong people. There's a huge increase in inequality and an increase in corruption even beyond
what used to go on under the communist regime, which at least
was covert and did not therefore inspire imitation by the ordinary
people, who only dimly knew what was going on. Now everybody can see corruption everywhere. It's like the worst days of
the United States a century ago. The Russians have copied many
of the worst features of capitalism first, and one hopes it doesn't

take them a hundred years to get to the stage of law and order – to some kind of business ethic which we rely on in western economies.

My conclusion would be that we cannot deal with this in one dimension or in too short-term or medium-term economics. We need to look at the whole basis of civic society. Maybe we should put up front the aid which, I think, is going now to the Russian police force. We actually need to impose a system of law and root out corruption before anything else is going to work properly.

Cooper: I think it could be argued that if cheap credit is to be had, it will be had by the entrenched interests basically. Therefore, where you really want to move resources into other areas, the only way to stop giving cheap credit to the entrenched interests is to create a regime where that's not possible, and the anti-inflation rhetoric is designed – it has not succeeded, of course – to cut down the flow of cheap and easy credit. The other thing is, of course, that this is unpalatable to the public, so part of the platform for retaining authority has been that inflation had to be kept, not at zero or anywhere close to it, but well below the levels that it has reached.

If we were discussing this issue a year ago, we would no doubt talk about the question whether there should be a currency union in the former Soviet Union. We talked a little this morning about flexible versus fixed exchange rates, and Bob Mundell raised the thought experiment of breaking up the United States into twelve currencies that float among themselves. We actually have a realistic case of that. The former Soviet Union was a currency area that broke up into fifteen republics. Leaving aside the three Baltic countries, which decided to break away entirely, the issue for a year was whether the remaining twelve countries should keep a currency union and, if so, what the modalities of it should be. As for the IMF, one of its mistakes, I think in retrospect, was to hang on too long to the idea of a single currency union among the twelve republics. That is now a bygone. Each of the twelve has selected its own currency. To put at least a silver lining on what may or may not be a cloud, there is a great deal of material here for Ph.D. dissertations in coming years because we now have a variety of very diverse experiments, from the extreme currency-board type of arrangement of Estonia, for example, to pure fiat money, pure floating.

Mundell: I'd just like to make the comment that if the Soviet Union had broken up in 1950, these independent countries would have had an international monetary system to enter, and the issue of stabilization would have been much easier. It seems to me that the present international monetary arrangements haven't been of any help at all to the countries of the former Soviet Union or the newly independent countries in Eastern Europe. We now have a system of managed flexible exchange rates, if you want to call it that. What sense is there for the IMF to go over to Belarus or any of the independent countries and suggest that they have a flexible exchange-rate system? It makes no sense. I think it was much easier in the 1947–71 period when there was a stable numeraire for the other countries of the world economy. Countries might inflate a lot and might have to devalue a lot, but there was at least that central tendency in the world economy.

I think the IMF is not now serving its purpose. It has become simply a statistics-gathering agency and a consulting agency – a vast consulting agency – and it provides advice like any other consulting agency, sometimes good and sometimes bad. It's not the staff of the IMF that's at fault for the present situation; it's the countries that created the existing arrangements. There's a vacuum here. The quality of the advice that's given to countries by the Fund is poor, and it's poor in large part because of the lack in the world economy of an international monetary system. We're going to talk about that later, so I won't mention any more about it now.

Corden: On Bob's point just now, I would say the answer is that the dollar is available and the Deutsche Mark is available, so if countries were able to get their budgets under control, they could, if they wanted to, peg to the dollar or the Deutsche Mark, just as in the Bretton Woods era they would have pegged to gold. But you have to remember that even in the Bretton Woods era there were certain countries, notably Argentina and Chile, that couldn't get their budgets under control, and had high inflation. So the availability of a fixed anchor doesn't ensure that a country has the political capacity to adhere to it.

That's just a small point. On the more general Sachs thing, I've heard him talk many times, and it all sounds very convincing. And then I say to myself, what he's really asking for is that the developed countries provide large sums of money to a country in a state of gross disorganization, where it is impossible to guide the funds in any rational way unless they're precisely targeted. I can understand the idea of providing funds for specific purposes – for example, for nuclear disarmament or for improving the nuclear reactors; something very precise and specific.

Cooper: Which is being done.

Corden: Yes, exactly, or for providing pharmaceuticals for hospitals. But this generalized aid; we've been through all this with other countries. You're asking massive aid for a country where so many of the population are simply not yet ready to accept elementary changes in policies that anybody from the outside can see are necessary. I'm really not convinced by all this.

Cooper: Well, I think, to put it a little unkindly perhaps, there is an élitist view of the world. You can take a small group of people whom you judge are on balance doing the right thing but who do not have wide public support, and you can bribe the public to support them for long enough for them to put the policies into effect. Sachs makes the analogy from time to time with the Marshall Plan. I think that is a false analogy. Perhaps a better analogy would be South Korea in the early 1960s, where again, to put it ungenerously, one could make the same kind of statement that I just made – that the US did provide money to bribe the Koreans to do some things that in the short run seemed to be unpalatable, but in the long run laid the basis for a fabulous thirty subsequent years.

Corden: The sums of money involved for the great Russian nation with its 180 million people are in a different category from helping Korea or the Czechs or the Poles. I think the west can make a significant impact on a country like Poland, for example, but can it really make a significant impact in this major reform in Russia?

Solomon: Speaking of the Marshall Plan, I can imagine people back in 1946, referring to the mess in Europe and the raging inflation in some of those countries, saying, 'Is there any point in pouring money into these countries in the hope that they will somehow straighten themselves out?'. I suppose there were people who held that view.

Cooper: You don't have to imagine people saying that; people did say that.

Solomon: So maybe there is something to the Marshall Plan analogy.

McCracken: I think this may be the same point that was made earlier, but I wonder if we aren't too much inclined to self-flagellation here. Jacob Viner about fifty years ago, when asked what our China policy ought to be, said, 'I have no idea, but I will confidently predict that, later on, you will decide that what you did was wrong'. It seems to me that was almost inevitable here, when you stop to think of the gargantuan problem of trying to take a large economy based on a totally different system and with no understanding of a lot of things that we would consider elementary. I should think that we could confidently predict that about now we'd be seeing a lot of articles that apparently we didn't do it right.

9. Observations on the So-Called Third World

Introduced by Robert Solomon

Chairman Cooper: Since yesterday morning, we've discussed at considerable length the current macroeconomic problems of a large part of the world. We have looked at North America – particularly the United States but also Canada to some extent – as well as Japan, Western Europe, the former communist countries of Eastern Europe and the former Soviet Union. It's time now to take a look at the problems of the rest of the world. Bob Solomon has agreed to lead the discussion.

Solomon: Well, let me say some words about what used to be called the Third World – the developing countries. I think one interesting observation is that during this recession in the industrial countries of the west in the last three or four years, the developing countries as a group have grown by something like 4 or 5 percent per year on average. The growth rates have varied in different developing regions – much faster in East Asia than elsewhere, as we know. Two things stand out. Number One, these countries were not forced into recession by the recession in the industrial countries. Number Two, the current-account deficit of the developing countries as a group has increased by a very significant amount during this recession. If you want to think of it this way, you can say that in some sense the developing world has been a locomotive for the industrial world during the recession; the recession would have been deeper in the industrial world without the increase in investment and exports in the industrial countries as a group, the balance-of-payments part of it being made possible by the large increase in capital flows to developing countries for all sorts of reasons.

Part of the reasons get to the third point I was going to make – that you've had some very significant economic reforms in a number of developing countries. You all know about Mexico, which has had a great deal of publicity in the last few months. A lot has happened there to open up the economy – to restructure, to deregulate, to privatize. Something very similar is happening in Argentina and elsewhere in Latin America. India, starting more recently, has an economic reform movement in which a tremendous amount of deregulation is going on. It has a long way to go, but there's a big start there, and it's an impressive development. We all know about the Four Tigers or Dragons, whichever you want to call them, of Asia in which all of this reform started much earlier, but they've been joined by Indonesia, by Malaysia, by Thailand, all of which are industrializing.

These are important changes in the world. I haven't mentioned the Middle East. Of course the OPEC countries are not doing very well. The price of oil is way down, and there is even a little retrenchment going on in Saudi Arabia and elsewhere. In what has been called the 'Continent of Woe' – sub-Sahara Africa – per capita income has been falling for the past two decades. I have very little to say about it except that it's a sad case. Dick asked me what the major issues are. I don't come up with any except to report these mainly favorable developments. But I may be missing something.

Corden: Well, I come in with major issues. One of the main facts is the movement toward liberalization, notably in Mexico, Argentina, Brazil, India to a limited extent, and of course China. Now the main implications for us are twofold. First, if it keeps going, apart from being very welcome, it means we have to be prepared to accept their goods. We have to make sure our market's there. There's going to be a continual challenge, I think, to the developed countries to adjust to the labor-intensive products coming from the developing world and not to respond with the normal instinctive response of protectionism. And just because the Uruguay Round is finished doesn't mean that this protectionist response isn't available, because you've got to remember the anti-dumping duties – the great new method of getting old-fashioned protectionism.

My second point is that we shouldn't assume that this liberalizing tendency is firmly embedded. There are still opponents and critics in many of the countries that I'm familiar with. The more we in the west go protectionist and produce protectionist philosophies and theories, the more we will influence the thinking of the developing countries in an adverse way, because it's the example of our own free-market approach, broadly speaking, that has helped them move the way they have.

Cooper: Maybe I could just add to Bob Solomon's observations of recent developments. We have just completed the Uruguay Round, and one of the features that marked the Uruguay Round is different from the Tokyo Round and the Kennedy Round – not only the scope, which is very much larger, but the active participation of many developing countries in this round. They recognized that the developed countries were asking things from them unlike the previous rounds, in which they said, 'No, we're foreign, we're developing, therefore there should be non-reciprocity'. This time they said, 'We will play, but you should recognize that we have some interests in playing'. One of them was agriculture, and some of these countries were lined up with the United States in opposing the agricultural policies of the European Community and Japan. Another interest was textiles, in which they were critical of the policies of both the United States and the European Community, and were able to get, if it's actually carried out over ten years, a complete transformation of the world textile regime. So this is a new element on the world scene, in which developing countries, instead of asking for exceptions so that they can be more protectionist, have taken an active interest in the world trading regime, and are willing to make commitments on their side in exchange for concessions which they received.

Willett: I would be interested in anyone's comments on the current state of the international debt crisis. This is not an area I work in a great deal, but in some sense the problem seems to have just gone away to some extent or at least the concern about it. How well was the debt crisis handled, and what might have been done better?

Frankel: To put Tom's question a little more pointedly, was the Brady Plan a turning point? The economics profession went through a certain cycle, I think, of initially after 1982 buying the view that it was a liquidity problem rather than an adjustment problem. And then, turning around, speaking of broad trends, I think a majority – Jeff Sachs is relevant here – were talking about writing down the debt – reducing the debt – saying that the main problem was that the debt overhang was inhibiting investment in these countries, and that wasn't in anybody's interest. Now it's sort of an open question. One view is that the Brady Plan was a move in that direction and that it was tried most successfully in Mexico. And I have heard one or two people claim that, yes, that's right, that it works, and that it was a key part of why the debt crisis is over.

Mundell: The same is true of Brazil.

Frankel: The clearest view that the debt crisis is over is, of course, that money is flooding into all these countries.

Solomon: That's the main point.

Cooper: Except for Africa.

Frankel: Even Egypt. Since we wrote down Egypt's debt, money has been flowing into Egypt – and into Lebanon and Jordan, of all places.

Cooper: The question is – and I don't know the answer – whether money is flowing in a way that one could plausibly argue that it was settlement of debt. One should be able to sort that out statistically. With respect to Mexico, I would say that the numbers suggest that there wasn't much in the Brady Plan that was real, so that to put weight on the Brady Plan would be putting a lot of weight on the psychological dimension rather than the tangible financial dimension. That doesn't mean that it's unimportant, but just gives a different emphasis.

Frankel: I have one more thought. I have read two retrospective stories on the lessons learned from the debt crisis, one by Jacques de Larosière and one by Larry Summers. De Larosière's lesson was, broadly speaking, that the original strategy was correct and it worked, and Summers' lesson was that the original strategy was wrong and that when we abandoned it things got better.

Solomon: They're both partly right.

Corden: It seems to me that there have been two factors operating. One is the changes in domestic policy that help to restore confidence. That is one of the main reasons for the movement of funds back into Argentina and Mexico. The other factor is the easing of the debt crisis, partly because of the Brady Plan. If I could just mention the order of magnitude with regard to Mexico, the reduced debt service resulting from the Brady Plan is between 1 and 2 percent of GDP. And only a limited number of countries were significantly affected by the plan: Costa Rica, the Philippines, …

Cooper: [interrupting] Costa Rica, the Philippines, Venezuela and Argentina, unless there's been a recent one that I'm not aware of. I think only five countries were actual beneficiaries of the Brady Plan.

Solomon: There may be a couple more now.

Corden: With three countries, there has been a big inflow of capital: Argentina, Chile and Thailand. And there it's completely domestic policies as the explanation. A huge transformation of the budgetary situation took place in Mexico. A huge reverse transfer of resources also took place, and it has taken years to bear fruit. Even now, the growth rate in Mexico is not particularly high.

Frankel: Let me add a third hypothesis on the table as to why there's a turnaround. The first was the write-down, the second was domestic policies. A series of papers from the IMF say that the main source of the huge reflow of capital into Latin America, East Asia and elsewhere is none of the above, but is the fall in the rates of return available in the United States and industrialized countries generally, due to the recession and the fall in interest rates, making the rates of return much more attractive in these other places.

Johnson: I thought it might be interesting just to cite the latest IMF figures showing the enormous change in the composition as well as an increase in the amounts of capital flows to developing countries. The figures show that the flows are much more equity-related, financial-market related, than they were before, so that foreign direct investment is now 18 percent of the flow. Portfolio equity is 6 percent, and that's risen from almost nothing. Bonds, which used to be quite unissuable by any developing country are now 10 percent, and bank loans, which used to be the mainstay, have now dropped to under 10 percent. These were over 40 percent ten years ago, and I think the lesson is that the banks – you know, once burnt, twice shy – are not going back in there, having got away with a bit less damage to their balance sheets than they might have feared in their worst fears. Suppliers and export credits, quite important, are at 16 percent; there's been a rise in those. Official loans have been remarkably stable at 29 percent, although of course in absolute amount they have risen. So the official sector has not backed out of this; official grants, at 11 percent, don't show much change.

I think it's quite interesting that the commercial banks are no longer major players. They still have quite a large stock of existing debt, but they're not putting a lot of new money in. These are still high-risk countries. Even when they're doing well, there's still the risk that something will go wrong. This is a prime case for equity-related investment, either portfolio or, more often, by large multinationals which are hoping to make big profits.

If I could just make a final comment slightly unrelated to this, it is quite clear that the developing countries which major in exports of manufactured goods have for some years done better, and will continue to do better, than countries which rely on commodity exports. The manufactured goods add more value; also, of course, the international price level of manufactures is much more stable. It's as stable as the US price level itself, while the price of commodities yo-yos up and down in the most disconcerting way – even more so than the price of currencies, which is saying something.

Cooper: I think an implication of the figures that Christopher has just read to us is that if it should happen, not this year, but in, let's say, two years, the rest of the world recovers and we see a substantial increase in short-term interest rates associated with that, the vulnerability of the Third World today is much less than it was twelve or thirteen years ago when interest rates went up so sharply. These portfolio flows sound as though they're much less sensitive to interest rates – short-term interest rates anyway – than bank loans, which were readjusted every six months.

Corden: The other big distinction from the 1970s and early 1980s is that the funds are going to the private sector and not to the government or to public-sector enterprises.

Cooper: I'm not sure how much comfort we can take from the fact that it's to the private sector. That was also the case in Chile, in Argentina and in Mexico, where substantial portions, not all, but substantial portions of the debt were to private-sector enterprises and where, with different mechanisms in all three cases, the public sector ended up in absorbing what had started out to be private debt. So the flow to the private sector doesn't provide as much security as it might in a stable industrialized country, for example. At least it didn't in the past.

Solomon: While we're listing favorable factors, not all the capital that's flowing in is being spent. These countries in the aggregate have been accumulating reserves in rather substantial amounts.

Cooper: So they're borrowing at 5 percent and lending at 3 percent.

Solomon: Well, they probably are, but the reserves would provide some sort of cushion if there is a falloff in capital inflow later on.

Mundell: Let me just underline what Dick was saying about lending to the private sector. In Uruguay, let's say in 1981, the Citibank had lent on mortgages something like $150 million. The mortgages were collapsing, and foreclosure was about to take place. Then the government passed a law stating that no foreclosures of mortgages could be done for a period of two years. As a result of that, the head of Citibank in Uruguay and I worked up a deal by which a mortgage bank in Uruguay took over the debts, and the central bank lent the money to the mortgage bank, which paid the Citibank.

It seems to be a general law that developing countries borrow until they're no longer good credit risks, at which time they have to stop borrowing, so we have another debt crisis. The crisis of the early 1980s is over, but debt is building up again to a level that may work, but is storing up problems for the future. A lot of good things are happening in Mexico, and these assets probably will all be okay if the world economy keeps growing well. What really caused the debt crisis in the early 1980s was the big, deep recession in the United States. And if the United States again turns into some kind of recession, then all those debts are going to be problem debts so far as the banks are involved.

Cooper: Let me try to tie this discussion to some things that were said yesterday. Let's suppose that Bob Solomon has adequately characterized what's happening in at least many parts of the world, and let's suppose further that this continues for some time; it's not just a flash in the pan, but the reforms continue, and they are successful in the sense of leading to more efficient production, increases in output and more rapid growth in the developing countries. Let's suppose further that their borrowing capacity or their capacity to import capital – not just borrowed capital – continues to grow because they are doing well both in reality and because the policies are acceptable to investors around the world. We don't have to suppose that they're going to be quite as spectacular as South Korea and Taiwan were over the last thirty years in order to see a tremendous rate of increase of production and presumably of exports of manufactured goods of all kinds – light manufactures in the first instance.

Now yesterday, Paul Samuelson raised the theoretical possibility – but, as I heard him, he went further and suggested that even if it were not an accurate characterization of the past, it would be of the future – that this prospect would not only blunt the growth, but might actually reduce real per capita income in the currently rich countries. I would like to put that possibility on the table and ask for your individual judgments on what exactly are the implications for the rich countries: Western Europe, North America, Japan. The Eastern European countries, or what are now called Central European countries, which are potentially in the same situation – Poland, the Czech Republic, Hungary – are undertaking major economic reforms. It's too early to pronounce in their cases smashing success, but some of the early indicators are positive, and there's a reasonable prospect that they will be successful, in which case they should also join the successful developing countries. What about it? Is this a bad thing or a good thing for the Americans, the Europeans and the Japanese? Do you want to distinguish between Americans, Europeans and Japanese? Or is it a big yawn – it doesn't make much difference one way or the other? This is at least potentially an extremely important issue for the next two decades, and may dominate at least one dimension of politics in these countries.

Samuelson: I just want to comment on one aspect of that problem. I spoke yesterday, somewhat tongue in cheek, about how marvelous we Americans are and what a stellar pattern we set for the rest of you, particularly the Europeans. I wouldn't want to exaggerate that as true, but let me say in seriousness that to the degree that we face the problem you've described, I think America's institutions may be at a better stage and state to meet them than European institutions. I'm not sure about Japan, because we don't know which way Japan is going.

I once talked at MIT to a vast number of trade-union leaders, and I said many things that they liked. And then I said, 'You know, unions are extremely important'. They all sat up, and I said, 'They're extremely important because they determine the speed at which industries die'. I had in mind the railroad industry. Well, in America these unions no longer have autonomous powers to determine the speed at which the coal industry dies, the railroad industry dies, the speed at which the textile and shoe industries died in New England, because the market has taken over. I don't know whether this process has arrived at the same stage in Europe, but I know as a prophet that it will. Employers today are constantly saying to the few unions that are left, 'You've got to concede this work method or we're going to have to close down'. Well, that's what happens in industrial life. If you don't make those concessions, if you can't make those concessions, you may end up not being there because the firm isn't there.

Uncle Tom and Booker T. Washington in the black community are objects of derision. But Uncle Tom was a very good worker in a way that many people, brought up in our modern urban centers, are not good workers. But I have been pleasantly surprised by the degree to which the American society has somehow accepted the unattractive jobs out of the market-clearing jobs that are there. Typically, when you're laid off in suburban Boston and you have had a $100,000 a year job, it takes at least a year to get your pride down. You use up your liquid assets, and you get back kind of a regression toward the mean; you get back to a job earning 30 or 40 percent less. Derisively, people say you've become manager of the local Burger King or McDonald's. Well, that's better than holding out to be Archbishop of Canterbury [laughter].

Johnson: On that point, this just came up this morning when Sven Arndt asked a question about what I expected from labor-market convergence in Europe. And one might broaden it to ask whether European labor markets converge towards American practice, which I think means much greater inequality, because the rewards justified by productivity now cover a much wider distribution in most advanced economies between the most highly skilled and the least highly skilled people. I think one of the important things is the abolition, or at least the tempering, of minimum-wage laws and the reduction of social-security contributions on low wages so that we can price more unskilled people, who are, I am afraid, the dropouts from our rather poor education systems – thus getting more marginal workers in part-time jobs, jobs that nobody else will do, non-unionized jobs. All these trends are very visible in Europe.

Cooper: Do you want to distinguish between Britain and Europe? You mean both?

Johnson: Well, I would say that Britain has led the European trend, but other countries are moving to modify things like minimum-wage laws, and some countries have moved further ahead than Britain – for example, making it possible for people to work shorter weeks for less money so that more people can work. All these kinds of things are happening, and are being encouraged. There was a notable White Paper by M. Delors of the European Commission, which after the British had mangled it a bit the British Chancellor of the Exchequer said it was quite a good effort – a paper about growth, competitiveness and employment, describing these changes in labor patterns without actually citing the American model, but it's quite clear what he had in mind.

The flip side of this coin is that of course there has to be acceptance of greater inequality than we've been accustomed to. The old Swedish model that everybody could get a rather similar wage, and if they got paid more the tax system would redistribute it lower down. All that seems to have given place to a more unequal distribution of incomes and skills, with the possibility of social unrest and extremist parties, usually of the Right rather than the Left, trying to capitalize on the kind of discontent caused in this way.

Samuelson: Just one comment. Dividing the work into a shorter week per worker is a humane adjustment to a short-run situation. It does not do much for you in future real GNP per capita trends. It is settling for the inadequate effective demand for people to use your resources. In this country, we have a rather surprising phenomenon – that the work week for those who are part of the official working force, instead of secularly declining, is actually at a peak level. We need other kinds of adjustment to meet the problem that worries me.

Johnson: Well, can I just say that this kind of adjustment has been practised notably in Denmark and the Netherlands. The important thing is not to compel people to work shorter weeks if they want to work longer weeks, but to allow choice in the length of the working week – though not to pay people higher marginal wages for working overtime, because you give a wrong incentive for people to work longer than they really want to. That's wrong, and tends to squeeze out people who might otherwise join the labor force.

Frankel: I'd like to bring the discussion back to the Third World. I think it's worth recalling that the economic success of East Asia and other parts of the Third World constitutes a spectacular success for US policy and, more generally, western policy in the postwar period. In my own view, it's a more important factor for why we won the Cold War than Star Wars, let's say, or some of the other things that it's attributed to. I think it's worth recalling how important the example of these countries adopting what is essentially a capitalist system has been. And I don't think it's over.

Just stick to the political dimension for a moment. The victory is not complete. We have the possibility of right-wing nationalist backlashes and of moving away from the western system in central European countries in the former Soviet Union, and if we close up our markets now, that will be a sign that we think the rules of the game are very important as long as we're winning and they're losing, but as they start to do well, we change the rules. And that would not be received too well. Usually in the political debate in this country, everybody assumes that you're admitting it's not in the American economic interest. It turns out to be very difficult to argue that it's in our political interest and it's in our economic interest, but I believe that open markets are in our interest in both respects. I think the slowdown in US real income growth over the last twenty years is not due to trade; I think it would have been a little bit worse if we hadn't had the opportunity to buy goods more cheaply abroad where other countries have the comparative advantage, and the source instead is slow productivity growth due to inadequate investment in physical and human capital.

There is a real issue of the wage gap which has been widened rather substantially in the 1980s between skilled labor and unskilled labor. And certainly this is the most plausible explanation why the debate over NAFTA in this country got so emotional. It's a bit hard to explain otherwise. NAFTA was essentially the Mexican government unilaterally agreeing to remove its tariff barriers. It was very hard to understand the depth of the emotion and opposition among US labor unions and labor more generally, but it has to be this general anxiety and doubt about the ability of Americans to compete in the world, and NAFTA just happened to be the thing we were voting on.

The econometric studies I've seen – I would mention Larry Katz in particular – suggest that this widening wage gap between skilled and unskilled labor in the United States was not due primarily to international trade, which of course it could be. Standard trade theory says that the country as a whole benefits from trade, but if it's labor-intensive imports of course Samuelson says that unskilled labor would lose. The estimates are that, at most, 15 percent of the wage gap up until now is due to the foreign-trade factor. But I would not rule out the possibility. It seems quite possible that in the future more and more of this gap is going to open up and be attributable to international trade. But either way, it seems to me the solution is to invest in physical and human capital and training. Technology of course explains most of the gap. With or without international trade, for people who can use computers versus those who can't, and so on, the solution is to try to get those skills distributed as widely as possible in our workforce.

Tobin: Well, I think the main reason to be pessimistic about our own country, the United States, is the education system and its apparent failures, which are not entirely just the schools and the educational establishment – partly that – but the whole family situation and the community situation that doesn't support the schools to the degree that would be necessary to diminish the gap that Jeff was talking about. It would be difficult to raise a larger percentage of the American population to the degree of skill – not just skill in specific matters but generalized understanding and ability to operate – that would justify our wages relative to those in less-developed countries.

So it's a big challenge, and more important, I imagine, than physical capital for the future per capita income of this country. And since the various dimensions of this problem seem to be getting worse rather than better, that is a depressing thought – the breakdown of the family in many areas, all the problems of inner cities, and so on. That doesn't mean the suburban schools are doing all that great, though we probably do better than most countries with the upper 20 percent, but with the other 80 percent we don't, by any means. We don't seem to be prepared to spend the resources that are needed. Many of those resources have to go through public rather than private hands, and government is unpopular in the political sphere these days.

One of the most depressing stories I've heard in recent years was about the Nestlé Food Corporation, which puts up plants all over the world. The Nestlé people have different packages for investing in countries, depending on the degree of sophistication and organization which their technology will require with the local labor force – different ones for advanced countries than for the less-developed countries. And when they think about the United States, we get the less-developed country's package!

Johnson: I just have one two-handed comment on that, which is if you look at non-traded services, there is no reason why wages should equalize across countries. American government officials probably get paid ten times what Mexican government officials get paid, even though they may be of equivalent standards of education and doing exactly similar jobs. Because these services are not traded, it is not necessary to have factor-cost equalization, and because of considerations of fairness, service wages generally keep pace more or less with wages in the traded sectors of the economy.

Tobin: Well, in that case we have to do well in the traded sector in order to be able to pay the salaries of professors and government servants that you're talking about.

Cooper: And if the labor market is in the long run not segmented, you can't pay higher salaries in the non-traded goods sector than you can in the traded goods sector.

Johnson: I'm not saying higher, but as high.

Cooper: I know, but if the wages are equalized in the traded goods sector, then they are also going to be equalized in the non-traded goods sector.

Johnson: Well, we're talking about unit labor costs being equalized, not wages. You've got to look at the combination of wages and productivity.

Tobin: As you said or implied, it isn't that our professors and public servants are any more efficient in providing whatever services they do than those in the United Kingdom – and you might, in fact, think they're less efficient. So if we have to pay more, it's because the public sector and the service sector are competing with our trading sectors for the manpower and womanpower that are involved.

Samuelson: On this point. We have seen a dramatic reduction in the US saving rate relative to our past history. Part of that was predictable and predicted – for example, by the Modigliani life-cycle hypothesis. But the degree to which it has taken place, to my knowledge, was not predicted correctly by any earlier scholars. And it's extremely pervasive. It's understandable that an affluent country would feel inclined to save less, but this has entered not only into private family savings but into corporate saving, and the legacy of Reaganism is a very strong but correctable – at least in principle correctable – negative saving in the public sector.

Now I would submit that if a sociologist analyzes all of the things that have contributed to this reduction in thriftiness, it will also apply in the educational level. Marie Antoinette said, 'Let them eat cake', as her solution for poverty. Many of my economist colleagues say, 'Let them have human capital'. But you've got to get human capital, and one of the things you have to do in order to get human capital is to stay away from the TV screen. You have to do that rotten calculus. You have to submit to an unequal track system and all those medieval motivating tortures that used to prevail. It's noteworthy that if someone sells me gasoline at night – and it's very hard for me to find someone – it's an immigrant, not an American; it's a hungry person who has been here for only two or three years. And I think that's part of the trend which in principle we know how to correct, but people have to want to have the behavior patterns which people don't seem to want to have now.

Solomon: It might be interesting to note that the United States is not the only country where the savings rate has declined. Most industrial countries have experienced a decline in the savings rate in recent years. And most of them have also moved toward more government dissaving.

Samuelson: Right; and if a friend of yours is a visiting professor in Sweden, your child cannot be in a fast track, because that is regarded as vying. The deterioration of knowledge of foreign languages permits a textbook like mine to be translated into Swedish, where everybody in Sweden is supposed to know English. This is a modern phenomenon, so we can predict that these trends will take place, but, as is often the case, we in the United States are at the beginning of the line.

Tobin: One more remark on the security of our standard of living because of non-traded goods. Services are beginning to be internationally traded on a pretty good scale, so if you call up the 800 number of some insurance company to talk about your claim, you may find yourself talking to somebody in Ireland who is well educated and can do that kind of job more cheaply, and perhaps better, than the people one might hire in New York City.

Cooper: I would like to impose on Max Corden and Mr Wakatsuki to respond to a question I posed. I know Max has thought about it, and I think we would be interested in a Japanese perspective about the implications for standards of living in the rich countries of economic progress in the poor countries.

Cordon: It's clear that there are many aspects to this. The first point we might note is that there will be some sectors of the European Community – we've already talked about this – where the unskilled will in the direct sense probably lose from this, and one hopes they will be absorbed in the growth of the services sector and there will be justification for various policy actions to improve human capital adjustments.

That's one point. On the more general question, well, there is a theoretical framework that I suggested yesterday which seems to me to be appropriate. You take a given growth of foreign economies; you want to know if that's good or bad for us. The answer depends on the impact on our terms of trade. Will the terms of trade, say of the United States, improve or worsen as a result of this growth? Well, the first general point to make is that US trade is so diverse that there may well be no significant overall effect. Some relative prices will rise, and some will fall. The general presumption is that the relative prices of low-skilled kinds of manufactured goods will go down and of high-quality goods will go up because of the extra demand. And since the United States is an importer rather than an exporter of these low-skilled goods, there will be an improvement in the terms of trade.

If the foreign growth is unbiased, meaning that at constant prices demands and supplies of all goods rise in the same proportions, then we benefit from faster growth abroad. The faster the growth abroad, the more the terms of trade will turn in favor of us. That simple proposition – if it's unbiased, we benefit from foreign growth – must be qualified by the probability of some particular kinds of biases. As far as I can see, the biases, if anything, will be favorable rather than unfavorable, but that's one aspect of the story.

Another consideration is interdependent utility. I'm one of those old-fashioned, soft, liberal types who likes to know that there is less starvation in Ethiopia, and so the growth of developing countries will give me satisfaction because it will spread prosperity around the world. I think that should be put in the picture. The final consideration that I think is worth thinking about: will the security of the world improve or worsen as a result of this kind of growth? Well, here I must say that historical experience suggests that growth does not lead to stability, and very often the most dangerous countries are not the poorest countries nor the rich stable countries, but the countries that are in the process of moving upward. The changes in income distribution that inevitably take place in the process of growth, as would happen in India if it really gets moving, can create lots of tensions of various kinds and problems of instability, of terrorism, and so on. So I would think that this is probably a negative aspect of prosperity.

Samuelson: I would like to sharpen the analytical discussion. Broadly speaking, technological progress abroad in goods in which people abroad have had, do have, and will continue to have comparative advantage is an unmitigated benefit to us. And, broadly speaking, technological progress abroad in goods which previously the countries abroad did not have comparative advantage – in which we had comparative advantage – is going to be harmful to us through the terms of trade.

I think it would be very dangerous to think you could predict exactly where the frequency distribution of progress abroad is going to fall. By my back-of-the-envelope calculation, of the 50 percent increase in well-being of the typical American between, say, 1950 and 1970–75, I would have imputed half of that to be because of getting good things from abroad more cheaply. At dinner parties when we discuss why we're alive at this age, it turns out that there's some high-precision hospital equipment that is made in Japan, an antibiotic which is in vats in Puerto Rico, and when you add all this up into a good index-number welfare comparison, the bias, it seems to me, in the first part of the postwar period was in our favor – less so, I think, in the latter part of the period, but it's hard to be dogmatic.

I just want to finish with a semi-teleological consideration. Technological progress has not been random and exogenous, but is something that comes about as a result of profit-seeking human effort. Ask yourself this question, but don't make it too narrowly profit-seeking at the firm level: if you were advising one of these developing countries, and it has a limited amount of resources to throw into the first category of technological change that I described, which is technological change in goods in which it already has comparative advantage and will continue to have comparative advantage, or to use those same resources on the other side of the line – those goods in which it has a newly acquired comparative advantage – which would be most profit-able to the country? Now that's a very non-Adam Smith question. Nobody is ever supposed to say what's good for Scotland; they say, 'What's good for McAdam?'. But I'm asking the question, and I think you will see that it's a little bit better to throw your efforts with the limited resources in the direction of the kind of technological change which keeps its benefits of consumer surplus more nearly at home than splash them on undeserving Americans who already have an awful lot.

Cooper: I want to ask Mr Wakatsuki how this issue is seen from a Japanese perspective.

Wakatsuki: Well, this is a very difficult question to answer. We are now coming to a stage where we understand better how Americans and Europeans felt during the 1970s, 1980s and maybe still now about the strong growth of Japanese exports. So we are still in a very ambivalent position. We have the advantage of being surrounded by very high-growth countries – East Asian as well as Southeast Asian countries, China, and now possibly India. We regard these countries as opportunities rather than as a threat. When we look at the trade of the so-called 'Four Dragons' or 'Four Tigers', or whatever you want to call them, and other Asian countries, including China, recent statistics show that intraregional trade is growing very rapidly and that, for the region as a whole, its dependence on trade with the United States is declining.

Naturally, our capital outflow is in the form of direct investment. The capital movement has been like a flight of wild geese. First, there was the movement of capital to Japan. Then Japan invested in Korea, Taiwan and Hong Kong. Now these countries are investing in Thailand, and Thailand is investing in Indonesia and the Philippines. This kind of mutually accelerating process, I think, benefits the world as a whole.

Of course there are problems. Protectionist sentiment against Japan has become much stronger with the growth of Japanese exports to the western world. But the fact that this intraregional trade is growing faster than, say, Japanese exports to the United States may soften the sentiment of protectionism. Already we see that many European countries and the United States are looking at this region for new investment opportunities. And I think it should be that way.

Mundell: I just want to make a comment about the Samuelson argument on technological progress. I would put it this way – that technological progress in an import-competing industry in another country will hurt the partner countries, but in export industries technological progress helps a country in terms of comparative advantage. But this problem in some sense is self-correcting, because once a country gets up to a point where its technological progress gives it a comparative advantage, then all further technical progress in that industry helps the rest of the world. At first, let's say, the import-competing industry in India is automobiles. Then progress in that industry in India at first hurts the world's automobile exporters. But after India becomes an exporter of automobiles, then this helps the rest of the world.

Samuelson: Well, yes, to put it graphically, think of a line on the comparative advantage continuum – call it the Graham–Edgeworth line – that separates exports from imports. It's the technological progress which crosses that line, and which moves that line, that is harmful. Constantly, there is a process going on in which countries abroad are beginning to be the domicile of things which previously were in America. I think of the vast manufacturing sectors which were safely in the United States and are now done abroad, and I dramatize by saying Japan. Rochester hasn't produced a camera for years and years. Instead of the Christmas tree ornaments which I used to get from Japan and which stood for cheap, low-quality items, we now get all the high-precision stuff. Whenever I'm interviewed, I ask where this tape recorder came from, where that camera came from. It's that constant going over the line. Now it will be cold comfort when we have comparative advantage only in Christmas tree ornaments. From then on, we'll be benefited by material progress abroad. Of course I exaggerate.

10. Reflections on the International Monetary System

Introduced by Robert A. Mundell

Chairman Cooper: Let me turn in the half hour remaining to our final topic, which is the international monetary system. Bob Mundell is going to introduce the discussion.

Mundell: First a bit of history about the different types of international monetary systems, starting, let's say, in the nineteenth century. Up to 1870 we had a bimetallic system. That collapsed with the Franco–Prussian War, when France stopped convertibility. Then from about 1870–73 until 1914 we had a gold standard for much of the developed world and a silver standard for much of the rest of the world. The decades wore on, and countries moved increasingly on to the gold standard from the silver standard. The silver standard was inflationary, and the gold standard, partly because of the shift of demand to gold was deflationary until South African gold came onto the scene. After Austria–Hungary and Russia went onto gold in the 1890s, the world price level started to rise, the value of gold fell, and that got us up to 1914. With the outbreak of World War I, Europe went off gold, inflated in paying for war expenditures, and gold flooded into the countries that stayed on gold, mainly the United States. With the excess supply of gold in the world because of the countries that went off it, the value of gold fell in half, and the US price level doubled even though the United States stayed on gold during the war. Then, with the very deflationary postwar recession, prices came way back down again. I call the period 1914 to 1924 the anchored dollar standard, because the US dollar was the main or only currency on gold until 1924, when Germany stabilized the mark on a gold basis. In 1925 Britain went back on gold, as did France in 1927. This is the resumption of the international gold standard.

I went through this background, this little travelogue, because there is something I wanted to say on the British return to gold in 1925. I agree, of course, with the general consensus of everyone around the room, the conventional wisdom if you like, that Churchill and Montagu Norman made a mistake by going back to gold at the old prewar parity. But I think that was a minor error. I don't think this was the major interwar error; it's got too high a billing for that. Keynes thought the pound was overvalued by 10 percent. I don't think that 10 percent in the exchange rate makes that much difference in a sound international monetary system. The problem in the interwar period, as Gustav Cassel pointed out, was the undervaluation of gold, because in the early 1920s there was ample gold for the anchored dollar standard when the United States had most of the gold, but the price level in the 1920s was 35 percent higher than in 1914 and higher than the average for centuries. Thus there was enough gold for the anchored dollar standard when other countries were not on gold, but not enough gold for a general international gold standard. The result in the later 1920s was an excess demand for gold, creating deflationary pressure and leading to the stock-market crash in the United States, the collapse of sterling in 1931 and the Great Depression.

I might just point out there that Gustav Cassel is, I think, the only academic economist who predicted the Great Depression. If something wasn't done to reduce the demand for gold in the world, we were going to have a depression on a scale never before experienced. And he wrote this in 1928. When I read Paul Samuelson's discussion of Cassel in a recent article – he was writing about revealed preference and real demand theory in Cassel – I was glad to see that, because Cassel has been underrated by economists.

Well, I have gotten that off my chest. Now we go on. What's often called the Bretton Woods system wasn't really a system at all. The Bretton Woods charter didn't define what the actual international monetary system was to be; it only established a set of rules and procedures and a requirement that countries keep their exchange rates within a certain percentage of parity. But this was an arrangement that was again an anchored dollar standard – anchored to gold in a sense. The US dollar was the only currency tied to gold in any loose way, and gold after 1934 was no longer redeemable in the United States. It was convertible internationally, but the dollar wasn't redeemable in gold for American citizens, who were forbidden to hold gold. The gold prohibition in the 1930s I attribute partly to the puritan tradition in the United States. After Americans got rid of prohibition of alcohol, they began to feel guilty, and were quite willing to have another prohibition that prohibited people from holding gold [laughter]. That only got changed in 1975.

Samuelson: Only Canadians understand Americans [more laughter].

Mundell: Well, Canadians profited from prohibition. That's why so many beer and alcohol companies are so profitable and famous in Canada; they supplied the market that was no longer possible to be supplied in the United States – the bootleg market.

Now in the early postwar period, gold again was concentrated in the United States, which had about 70 percent of the world's gold stock. The first break in the system occurred in 1950. The United States lost a large amount of gold in that single year. But people weren't worried about it. Most informed people at this time regarded the gold outflow as a useful redistribution of the world's gold stock. But the outward gold movement from the United States rather steadily continued throughout the 1950s, 1960s and early 1970s After a slight rise in 1951 and 1952, the US gold stock fell from 664 million ounces at the end of 1952 to 276 million ounces in 1972.

During the 1960s there was considerable sentiment in favor of raising the official dollar price of gold. The first conference in our series, in January 1967, was on this subject. Sir Roy Harrod advocated raising the price of gold as a means of increasing international liquidity, which he strongly believed was inadequate. Jacques Rueff, the noted French economist, was in favor of doubling the price of gold, not as a means of increasing liquidity, but as a prerequisite for a return to a full-fledged kind of gold standard. Although the IMF Articles of Agreement authorized the possibility of a uniform change in the price of gold in terms of member currencies, such a move was not politically feasible for the United States. The two big gold producers in the world were anathema in this country: South Africa, which then had a racist social system, and the Soviet Union, then our adversary. In US official circles, the idea of raising the price of gold just couldn't be talked about, but, as someone said, the laws of economics came out anyway. Instead of the price of gold doubling or tripling, as it would have under an official reform, the price of gold went up ten times; in 1980 it went up temporarily by twenty times. So those arguments about helping the Soviet Union and South Africa – they were helped best by the big upsurge in prices in the free market after gold had been demonetized.

Well, from the breakdown of the anchored gold standard in August 1971, we moved on to an unanchored dollar standard. The dollar was used as a basis for pegging currencies, but this was an unanchored system, because the dollar was no longer convertible into gold. So other countries had the balance-of-payments discipline imposed by the need to convert their currencies into the dollar and to keep exchange rates fixed. It was a one-sided thing because the United States had no convertibility commitment. That system broke down in 1973, and was replaced by an official movement to flexible exchange rates or, if we like, currency areas, because there was already in this period the movement to create a separate currency area in Europe.

In 1985, with the Plaza accord, we moved toward the idea that the market exchange rates weren't doing the right thing. The Reagan policy mix of tax cuts combined with tight money had led to a soaring dollar which, by restraining exports and stimulating imports, was regarded as contributing to the large US trade deficit. The US administration wanted to get the dollar down, and got the G–5 countries together at the Plaza to talk it down, partly to ward off protectionist pressure in Congress.

So the dollar was allowed to fall. I call the system after 1985 the coordinated dollar. The system we're in is one of flexible exchange rates and currency areas. Now the idea of international monetary reform, which had been talked about all through the 1960s, was abandoned when the Committee of Twenty decided that it would let countries move on to flexible exchange rates. In fact, the wording of its announcement in June 1973 was that the Committee was going to abandon international monetary reform until countries had got their inflations under control.

There was a little talk of reform when James Baker was Secretary of the Treasury, especially after the Louvre accord, which had decided that the dollar had gone down enough. There was an attempt to keep some kind of de facto fixed exchange rates, or stable exchange rates, at that time, and there was a question then that comes up in any fixed exchange-rate system which isn't anchored directly to gold: how do you decide which countries should do the adjusting? Should the surplus countries expand or should the deficit countries contract? Under a gold standard, that's taken care of automatically, but under a discretionary system you have to make that decision. The basic idea that people talked about for a few months was that if there is general inflation in the world at a given level of stable exchange rates, then the deficit countries should contract; if there is deflationary pressure in the world, then the surplus countries should expand.

At the IMF meetings in September 1987, Secretary Baker made a big splash in the papers by saying that we must develop a commodity-price index, including gold, as a measure of inflationary pressure. And there was some support for this, but all of it collapsed with the stock-market crash in October. After that there was no longer any further talk on the subject. Under President Bush and Secretary Brady, there was zero talk of international monetary reform. Also, under the Clinton administration so far, there has been zero talk of international monetary reform, and I don't expect there to be any talk of international monetary reform during this administration.

Tobin: With respect to gold, I was strongly opposed to the controls and the buy-American kind of things we were doing in the 1960s to preserve the façade that we were still on the gold standard. And I don't like to be cast along with those people who thought it was terrible to raise the price of gold in 1933–34.

Samuelson: I'm glad to hear that you were on my side. I honestly did not realize that you were a stalwart on my side [laughter].

Tobin: Under President Kennedy, talking about any change in the value of gold or the dollar was to risk being beheaded by Robert Roosa [Undersecretary of the Treasury] the next time you met him at a party.

Corden: My problem is that I have absolutely no reminiscences to report, but let me talk very briefly about the present system. What are the characteristics of the present system? Well, Point One, we have very high and probably irreversible international capital mobility. That has two implications. First of all, we have large, varying current-account imbalances, which are not necessarily bad; the saving and investment considerations underlying them determine whether they're good or bad. Secondly, the high capital mobility makes it pretty well impossible to sustain a fixed but adjustable exchange-rate system. The result is that we have a managed floating system. The management has two aspects to it. Probably the minor aspect is official intervention; I'll leave that to Jeff Frankel to tell how minor or major that is. The major form of management is monetary policy. Each country mostly does its own monetary-policy management, taking into account domestic considerations and a little bit of exchange-rate considerations. And there is some modest degree of coordination, consultation, and so on. There was a brief period, essentially 1985 to 1988, when there was a significant amount of concerted intervention. And that seems to me the present system.

When we talk about reform, what do we mean? Do we want to change the international capital market? Well, it would be very difficult even if we wanted to. Do we want to change the exchange-rate system? In my view, the only serious alternative is full monetary union, the real thing – that is to say, what the Europeans are trying to do on a regional scale. And given the difficulties that the Europeans are having in bringing this about, I would think that full monetary union involving, say, the United States, Japan and Germany, is somewhat improbable. Therefore, we're going to continue with the present system.

Tobin: I agree with that completely.

McCracken: The participants here might be interested in the long meeting, which I attended, at Camp David in August 1971. At the end of the meeting, the president had decided favorably on all of the wrong things, but the meeting adjourned with his concluding that it was not wise to close the gold window. Before the night was over, however, he changed his mind.

Cooper: You're sure this was a change of mind and not just a standard presidential tactic of keeping his advisers in the dark, having heard their advice?

Samuelson: Just prior to that meeting, there was a request for gold from the English.

McCracken: That is correct.

Cooper: I would support that, but it must be said that the English had sold a lot of gold to the United States shortly before. So their view was that they were simply restoring the *status quo ante*. In the meantime, many countries in 1970 and 1971 purchased gold from the United States.

We're past the hour of five, and I think this is the proper time to bring the meeting to a conclusion. I will just say that I also agree with Max Corden's conclusion about the present system. Normatively, however, I think that it would be desirable to start thinking about the alternative, which Max says is politically impracticable. I think that twenty years from now, we will not be happy that folks at meetings like this did not discuss seriously what I agree is the only practical alternative to a floating-rate system. But that is a topic for another conference.

11. *Third Robbins Memorial Lecture** Is All That European Unemployment Necessary?

Robert M. Solow, Nobel Laureate in Economics

Sooner or later, there will be a Robbins Lecturer who has never met Lionel Robbins – in person, I mean, because there is no excuse for not knowing his work as a scholar and public person. Anyway, that day has not yet come, although I probably had no more than six or eight conversations with Robbins altogether. I spent two full academic years in England during the 1960s, but they were 1963–4 in Cambridge and 1968–9 in Oxford – never in London. I met Robbins when I visited the London School of Economics to give a talk or attend a seminar, or occasionally somewhere else. He was unfailingly amiable and animated, with none of the air of inattention with which I imagine the Duke of Portland would have talked to one of the lesser knights of his domain. Of course, if Lionel Robbins had chosen to adopt that manner, he would have carried it off with infinitely more skill than any Duke and left me completely fooled. But I do not think that was it. He was a good conversationalist because he cared about ideas.

On the other hand, he was courtly. Lionel Robbins could no more have appeared uncourtly than Wilt Chamberlain could have appeared untall. I did rather feel like a schoolboy when I was with him. But then I suppose I was. In any case, I have no quaint anecdotes about Lionel Robbins to tell you. I do have one story that I want to tell because it has some relevance to the subject of

*Public lecture delivered on the eve of the conference.

this lecture. Unfortunately, I cannot remember how I came by this story, but it is so clear and definite in my mind that it must be true.

There was once a man named Arthur Salter, a very high Treasury civil servant and the author of the most boring autobiography I have ever read. It covers the Great Depression of the 1930s, when Salter was active (if that word could ever be used of him). Reading autobiographical accounts of the Thirties by important public policy players of the time – even Hugh Dalton's to take a much more interesting person – is almost scary. It is so obvious that they were all clueless about the Depression. They could not even begin to think about what was happening to them and to everyone. One is reminded of General Westmoreland's memoirs of the Vietnam War – the story of a bullfight as told by the bull – except that the Depression was not a contest between two sides but an impersonal disaster. The autobiographical accounts reflect deep incomprehension.

Anyway, the story is that, long afterward, Arthur Salter ran into Lionel Robbins, in a club no doubt, and harrumphed that when all is said and done we really knew what we were doing in the Thirties. To which Robbins replied, in effect: 'No, Salter, I have to admit that I was dead wrong about many things then, and I do not remember that you were in any way better'. That was admirable. We often speak of 20–20 hindsight as if it were easy to come by. It is not.

Now I turn to my real topic, and I have to begin by reciting some facts. In the fifteen years between 1959 and 1973, we in the United States used to wish that we could understand and perhaps imitate the secret that allowed the major European countries to manage their economies with so little unemployment. During those years, the US (and Canada) averaged 4.8 percent unemployment rates. In contrast, France had an unemployment rate of 2.3 percent, Germany 0.9 percent, and the UK 2.0 percent. The whole of the European Community averaged 2.3 percent and the EFTA countries 1.3 percent. They seemed to know something that we did not know.

In the decade of the 1980s, the story was altogether different. The unemployment rate in the US was a not so glorious 7.3

percent on average, though it peaked early in the decade and fell steadily from 9.7 percent in 1982 to 5.3 percent in 1989. But during the same ten years, the unemployment rate ran at 9.6 percent in France, 7.5 percent in Germany (eight times what it had been), and 10 percent in the UK. Canada was right up there at 9.8 percent, just to show that the Atlantic Ocean was not to blame. The European Community average was 10.1 percent, but the EFTA countries, though worse off than in the 1960s, had an unemployment rate of 3.3 percent.

The beginning of the current decade has merely continued the contrast. Although we lament our 'jobless recovery', and rightly so, we are still doing better than Europe and Canada. Unemployment peaked in mid-1992 at 7.7 percent, and has been falling slowly since then, reaching 6.4 percent in December 1993. Canada has averaged over 10 percent, and has recently been at 11 percent. The main European countries have not traced out a uniform history. The UK has improved a bit, France has got a little worse and Germany varies. Finland, of all places, has had a macroeconomic disaster, with the unemployment rate in the high teens; and Sweden, after decades of 2 percent unemployment and active labor-market policy, is flirting with unemployment rates at 8 percent or even higher. This role reversal has European economists and policy-makers wondering what *our* secret is. How do we create jobs when they find employment stagnating or falling, even as aggregate output is slowly rising?

This recital can be verified and reinforced by a more systematic analysis of the data. In almost every European country, large or small, the time series of unemployment rates appears to have a statistically significant upward trend beginning about 1974. For some the slope is shockingly large: a quarter of a percentage point per year in France and Belgium and Denmark, a little less but still there in Germany, and even more than a trace in Switzerland, to my surprise. The US is not immune either. The same mechanical data analysis says that the unemployment rate averaged a trendless 5.3 percent until 1974, when it began to trend upward at a tenth of a point a year.

I have called this mechanical data analysis because I mean it as just a shorthand description of the facts. I would not suppose that such a statistical trend in the unemployment rate has any analytical reality. When unemployment rises, there is a reason; reverse the reason and unemployment will fall. Time trends suggest Fate, and Fate has more important things to worry about than the unemployment rate. The question we have to discuss is precisely why Europe has experienced persistently higher unemployment rates since the mid-1970s and whether anything can be done about it.

There is a standard diagnosis of this episode of high and persistent unemployment, and it seems to be believed by most of the press, by many economists, and by all public officials and central bankers. Nor do I think it is all wrong. You would be properly suspicious of me if I did; the odds are that any particular claim to be the Messiah is overblown, to say the least. But I do think that the standard diagnosis is only about half-right – maybe 60 percent at the most – and the other 40 or 50 percent is very important, for a reason that will become clear.

The standard diagnosis is that all of this drift to higher unemployment is the result of labor-market rigidities of various kinds. Employers are discouraged from hiring workers for reasons that are internal to the labor market, having to do with the nature of the employment contract, with regulations that limit the employer's flexibility in meeting changing business conditions, and with taxes and social charges that drive up the cost of labor to unreasonable and unproductive heights. To the extent that this analysis of the unemployment problem is right, drastic consequences follow for the design of economic policy. To begin with, the implication is that high unemployment is not a macroeconomic problem, and the agencies responsible for macroeconomic policy are off the hook. Naturally, then, the view that I have described appeals strongly to central banks and ministries of finance. It gives them what everyone wants: dignity without responsibility. And this is in fact the prevailing mood.

The second consequence, of course, is that the proper course of action is to make the labor market more flexible by undoing the rigidities and regulations that have created the problem in the first place. That is a delicate and difficult matter because many of those regulations and rigidities were intended to serve a social purpose, and may actually do so, but with unintended side effects. I do not want to tackle that set of issues, if only because to do so intelligently would require a better grasp of local social institutions and attitudes than I am likely to have. It is enough for my purposes to remind you that any such approach to policy is drenched in politics, not just barnyard politics but the politics of the social contract. If anything constructive can be done in this field, it will be done very slowly. So once again the implication is that nothing can be done, at least not soon.

It would take too much time to survey the details of the standard diagnosis, but I want to be a little more concrete, especially because I think it is an important part of the true story. One tricky element, for example, is the prevalence in Europe of laws and regulations that make it very difficult for a firm to lay off or discharge workers when the market goes sour, either secularly or cyclically. There are requirements for advance notification, sometimes many months in advance. There are provisions for severance pay lasting as much as a year. And there are procedural requirements that make for hassle and sometimes for paralysis. The goal, naturally, is to provide workers with some job security and with some protection against casual discharge for no good reason. Many Americans, including some professors of economics with tenure, find this unreasonable or even incomprehensible. I am not among them. But the result in practice is that firms are reluctant to hire workers even when business is pretty good because they foresee high cost and much inconvenience when economic conditions worsen, as eventually they will. So employment stagnates even when business turns up.

Another characteristic of European industrial relations is the fact that a large and generous social-security safety net is financed very largely from charges on payrolls. We all know that the ultimate incidence of those social costs may be primarily on workers, but that is not the relevant point. In most European countries, the tax wedge between the cost of an hour of labor to the employer and the take-home pay of the worker can be as much as half of the full cost. In other words, the worker receives as wage only one dollar for every two that the employer pays out. The result is that the marginal cost of labor is very high, and this is especially the case for unskilled labor. Here too the intention is good; there is no intrinsic merit in an insecure life. But the unintended side effect is to make every hiring decision costly and risky, and especially for workers without advanced skills. The safety net itself has the additional effect that it drives up the reservation wage, again especially for unskilled workers.

Finally, it is worth mentioning that geographic mobility in the New Europe is still not great, and this is unlikely to change soon. Mobility across borders is of course limited by differences of language and culture. Even within countries, recent tightness in the housing market has made mobility very costly for workers. Thus local labor-market imbalances are likely to persist for longer than they would in a more mobile society like our own. And since a change of industry may often require a change of location, geographic immobility translates easily into industrial rigidity.

By the way, I have made it sound as if government regulation is the main source of labor-market rigidity. That is rather Colonel Blimpish. Some of what I have described is indeed traceable to regulation and taxation. But a lot of it comes from social norms and customs and some from trade-union pressure that in turn reflects norms and customs. That should not be forgotten in case anyone thinks that this is a situation that could be easily altered.

It is fair to say, as I did earlier, that this account of high and persistent unemployment is widely accepted in Europe, especially officially, as the true story and guide to policy. Within the economics profession, this acceptance takes the form of more or less elaborate assertions that the 'natural rate of unemployment' must now be somewhere in the neighborhood of 8–10 percent. After all, many countries experience unemployment rates this high with fairly stable inflation; the doctrine says that inflation can be stable only if the current unemployment rate is around the natural rate. Any schoolboy can see the implication. This is our way of saying that only the sort of structural change that alters the fundamental operations of the labor market can safely improve the situation.

I have never found this theory convincing. But all I want to do now is to argue that, whatever its general merits, it is not plausible as a complete explanation of the current situation in Europe, at least not by itself. The simplest and strongest evidence against it is the timing of events. The pattern differs a bit from one country to another, and the details may contain clues. But the following piece of potted history involves no important distortion as far as I can see.

Some slight upward creep of unemployment may have begun in the early 1970s, especially after 1973. It amounted to very little until 1978 or 1979. But then, in most of the large and small countries of the European Community, there was a concentrated rise in unemployment, almost a step increase. In France the unemployment rate went from 4 percent to almost 10 percent in the space of five years, and it has never really come down. In Germany the initial step was a little more pronounced, but then unemployment rose from a little over 3 percent to 8 percent in three or four years. There have been fluctuations since, but around a noticeably high level. Belgium, Denmark, Ireland, you name it: the picture is roughly the same. The story in the UK is more complicated, but basically similar. Before the second oil shock, unemployment fluctuated around a level no higher than, say, 4 percent. By the early 1980s, 9 or 10 percent was more like it.

You may wonder how this squares with the trend figures I was quoting a few minutes ago, with the unemployment rate going up at a couple of tenths of a point per year. That was just malicious. It gives me an opportunity to point out how misleading simple, cheap curve-fitting can be. If you tell the computer to fit a bunch of straight lines, that is what it will do. In the old days, when running a regression meant hours hunched over a desk calculator, one looked at the graph of a time series and thought twice, which is twice more than seems to happen nowadays.

Anyway, the picture I have just sketched does not fall naturally into the simple one-way causal story about labor-market rigidity.

The welfare state, the large tax wedge between labor cost and wage-packet, the immobility of labor, and all that did not happen in a few years after the oil shock of 1979. While it is not impossible, it is certainly far-fetched to claim that the slow build-up of rigidities could pass some threshold in the late 1970s, so that a long-term cause could translate into a sudden effect.

It is much more plausible to suppose that the long-term evolution of labor-market rigidity accounts for a slow rise in equilibrium unemployment and that another, additional, source of unemployment was superimposed on it some time in the late 1970s. This interpretation is confirmed by the observation that unemployment rates remained stable or perhaps rose or fell slightly even after some of the standard causes of labor-market rigidity were tempered in the late 1980s and early 1990s, as with the tightening and reduction of unemployment insurance benefits in some countries. If the sudden jump in unemployment in the late 1970s were entirely a response to labor-market rigidity, then the reversal that occurred later on should have brought more visible results than it did. Common sense suggests that the supply-side causes of unemployment work gradually. So there must be an additional causal factor to account for the actual course of events.

One does not have to look very far for it. The other thing that happened as the 1980s began was a nearly universal shift to tight macroeconomic policy, in a natural reaction to the acceleration of inflation after the second oil shock. In most countries, this took the form of tight monetary policy and high nominal interest rates. As the anti-inflationary medicine took hold, high nominal rates were converted into further increases in real interest rates. So a dose of demand-side-induced unemployment was added to the pre-existing level. It is no strain on the imagination at all to believe that this additional dose of unemployment could manifest itself in the space of a couple of years. So I want to suggest that the European economies have been living with a base of structural unemployment topped up with a substantial amount of unemployment that can be traced to inadequate aggregate demand. Tight money has won the battle against inflation, at least for now. But it has left behind a demand-side mess in the labor market.

That still leaves a mystery. Why has this situation persisted so long? With the decline of inflation, why has unemployment not returned to some reasonable equilibrium level? I think there are two sets of reasons, one at the macroeconomic level and one more specific to the labor market. I will take them in turn, but only briefly.

Unemployment has persisted because nominal and real interest rates have remained high. I suspect that there is an analytical error at the root of this misjudgment. If I attend to the remarks made by central bankers, ministers of finance, and other government officials, I think I hear them saying that the absence of inflation is not only a necessary condition for a satisfactory macroeconomic state of affairs, but a sufficient condition as well. They seem to think that the *only* requirement of sound macro-policy is the suppression of inflation. The rest can be left to Nature.

They may have been encouraged in this belief by some economists, but it certainly fits in comfortably with the spread of the perception that activist governments make things worse no matter what they do. I do not want to discuss the general issue of the proper scope of government action in economic matters, not even in a Lionel Robbins Lecture, where it might be appropriate. But I will say that I think a preference for minimalist government ought to rest on something more substantial than the faith that a modern market economy will find its way to stable high employment in a matter of a couple of years if only inflation is kept at bay. The last decade or so in Europe is evidence against that optimistic belief.

There is a second strand to this analysis of persistent unemployment, forcefully stated most recently by my colleague, Olivier Blanchard, and resting on research by him, by me, and by many others. The real problem with the labor market is that it has a tendency to convert actual unemployment into 'equilibrium' unemployment. There is a lot of interesting academic economic theory behind that assertion, but I will try to translate it into everyday terms.

Imagine that a national economy experiences a drop in employment for some simple demand-side reason, say a fall in exports not offset by a change in exchange rates. If the missing demand is replaced right away, from any source, employment will rise and go back to where it was before the initial shock. But, this argument says, if higher unemployment is allowed to persist for any length of time, the bearers of that unemployment start to lose their connection with the labor market. They become 'outsiders' and find ways to live without work, using a mixture of public and private resources. The longer they are unemployed, the less they are thought by potential employers to be eligible workers. For that reason they may search less intensively for a job, and this merely reinforces their status as outsiders in their own view as well as that of employers. This process shows itself statistically in the large – to an American, incredibly large – fraction of the unemployed in Europe who have been out of work for a year or more. That fraction is currently more than one-half. By comparison, in the US in 1983, after two years when the unemployment rate was nearly 10 percent, the median duration of unemployment was 10 weeks; half the unemployed had been out of a job for 10 weeks or more, as against 52 weeks or more in Europe.

This is not just a safety-net issue. The economic point is that the conversion of actual into equilibrium unemployment means that a given margin of unemployment exercises less pressure on the wage and other demands of employed workers. Similarly, it does less to stiffen the resistance of employers to all those things that we now describe as labor-market rigidity. Much more could be said about this, and Blanchard and others have said it. The upshot is that unemployment generated primarily by the successful containment of inflation can be said to look a lot like unemployment generated by sclerosis of the labor market. This reinforces the comfortable tendency for the makers of macroeconomic policy to announce that it is no longer their business. If there are any here who remember the songs of Tom Lehrer, I remind them that he wrote one about Wernher von Braun, the master of the buzz-bomb, who was imported into the US to practice his trade in the Cold War. According to Tom Lehrer: 'I send rockets up. Who cares vere dey come down? Dot's not my department, says Wernher von Braun'. There is something of a parallel here, and it is not a comfortable one.

I wish I knew with any confidence how much of the current level of unemployment in Europe is labor-market related and how much is aggregate-demand related. The right answer probably differs from country to country, as does the incidence of long-term (over one year) unemployment. I think reasonable answers could be found, country by country, but I do not know that the question has been asked by research workers. I do know that if you look closely at the record for the main European countries, you find that many of them showed no upward trend in unemployment at all before the mid-1970s. These include some, like Belgium and Denmark, and maybe even the Netherlands, that had pretty poor performances in the 1980s. France, however, did exhibit a statistically significant upward drift in unemployment from the 1950s on, perhaps as much as 0.15 percent per year. If you extrapolate at that rate from the mid-1950s to the present, you end up with the crude estimate that supply-side factors account for an unemployment rate of about 6 percent currently; thus as much as half of French unemployment may come from the demand side, and quite possibly more. I would not be surprised if that turned out to be a representative figure for the European Community generally.

Suppose there were a broad move in Europe to eliminate the demand-side unemployment by the obvious method, a policy-initiated expansion of aggregate demand. One must ask if there would be a substantial inflationary cost. It is possible that the conversion of demand-side to supply-side unemployment (as discussed earlier) has gone far enough that demand expansion would be met immediately with wage increases. But it is far from certain, and there is some experience to suggest that it is not the likeliest outcome.

For one thing, many countries have begun to weaken or dismantle the legislative and institutional obstacles to labor-market flexibility. I think that process should continue, within reason. I add the qualifying phrase seriously. The sort of Thatcherite – and not only Thatcherite – belief that the only good labor market is a

dog-eat-dog jungle strikes me as both socially wrong and economically unproductive. The safety net is there for good reasons,
and the reasons are getting better. Job security is not a bad thing.
It meets a human need; if there is some cost, that is what usually
happens when human needs are being met. No doubt it is possible for the welfare state to be carried too far; and that may
already have happened in some European countries. The goal
should be to find a comfortable and practical balance, not to
suppose that what horrified Hobbes is good for the rest of us. In
any case, the change of direction in recent years should have
provided some slack for a demand-side-induced rise in employment.

What about the possibility that the years of high unemployment have so segregated the labor market that the currently unemployed, and especially the half of them who have been out of
work for a year or more, have become unemployable? No one
can rule out that for sure, although it is surely significant that the
same claim has been made on other occasions, and has turned out
to be false every time so far. Business firms looking at profitable
sales opportunities can usually find a way to take advantage of
them, even if it involves hiring only entry-level people and up-
grading incumbent workers to slightly more skilled and responsible positions. That is the way it happened in the past, and one
might reasonably expect it to happen again.

So I would advocate a concerted steady expansion of aggregate demand in Europe aimed at eliminating a substantial margin
of unemployment, perhaps as much as 5 or 6 percentage points.
In the course of this exploration, we would no doubt discover
just how big that margin actually is. Europeans would then be in
a better position to think intelligently about the proper scope for
the welfare state and for guarantees of job security. One needs to
know where the margin is before one can make intelligent marginal adjustments.

Inflation in Europe is currently over 3 percent and not expected to go higher soon. If demand expansion were combined
with continued deregulation of labor and product markets, it is a
fair bet that several percentage points could be sliced from the

unemployment rate without significant enduring acceleration of inflation. A temporary bulge of a point or less would be tolerable because something important is at stake. Recent experience in the US has been consistent with that mildly optimistic assessment of the immediate potential for inflation, and many of the same forces are at work here and in Europe.

The belief that labor-market rigidity is the only significant source of unemployment has been a comforting alibi for policy authorities in Europe. Had the theory not existed, they might very well have invented it. This is not only because responsibility is generally burdensome. There is yet another reason why an aggregate-demand solution to the problem has seemed off limits: the commitment to fixed exchange rates embodied in the European Monetary System. There has been no shortage of voices calling for lower interest rates as a route to higher employment. (For well-known reasons, this does not seem like a good time to try expansionary fiscal policy.) Whatever theory one holds, that route has been closed off until very recently by the fixity of purpose of the Bundesbank. (Actually, there is one theory that does dissolve the problem. That is the theory that low and steady inflation will automatically cure the unemployment problem along with the common cold. No wonder it has been an attractive theory. If only it were true.)

God knows I do not want to open up this subject here at the end of a lecture. I will say only the minimum I need to say to get to the end of the lecture. For reasons having to do with the good or bad management of unification, the Bundesbank has believed that high interest rates were right for Germany. If they were wrong for the rest of the Community, that was not the Bundesbank's problem. Some breathing room could have been opened up for the other countries by an appreciation of the D-Mark within the EMS. The Bundesbank was prepared for that solution. The French government, which was playing a game that American boys call 'King of the Hill', was not. As a former American boy (or perhaps it should be American former boy), I can understand that. It did, however, paralyze European macroeconomic policy until Britain and Italy decided to abandon the game and eventually the EMS collapsed.

The way is now open to play a different game, perhaps with French leadership. Suppose that German interest rates do not come down fast enough to meet the needs of the rest of Europe. If France were to push its own interest rates down enough to induce a depreciation of the franc by, say, 5 percent, well within the new bands, and if Italy, Spain, Denmark and others were to follow suit, the D-Mark would appreciate by perhaps 3 percent in real terms. (In the course of this, France would have to make it clear to its partners that it was not seeking competitive devaluation against them.)

Appreciation of the D-Mark would change the terms of the debate in Germany, and properly so. German industry, facing a loss of competitiveness, would bring pressure on the Bundesbank. The appreciation would provide Germany with a free anti-inflationary ride. In this situation, the only argument against a reduction in German interest rates would be a reluctance to be seen to be following a French lead. If that obstacle could be overcome (notice that we are still playing King of the Hill), there is no reason why the process could not be repeated until real interest rates in Europe were reduced to a level appropriate to the widespread recession and the Continent's double-digit unemployment. John Flemming has pointed out that, once German investors saw what was happening, they would be led to move out of deposits and into bonds on which capital gains might be foreseen. Since bonds issued by banks are excluded from the monetary aggregates targeted by the Bundesbank, it could claim that its cooperation in a general reduction of interest rates was in fact called for by its own monetary policy directives. Everyone could at least pretend that their ideas had triumphed.

There are now definite signs of improvement in many European economies. In many of them, however, unemployment does not seem to fall. If there really is a tendency for prolonged unemployment to become 'structural' and to look 'natural', then it would be far better to eliminate as much of the demand-side-induced component as we can, while continuing to improve the functioning of the labor market. Otherwise, Europe risks creating a situation no one will like: the mainstream resentfully paying to maintain a large army of long-term unemployed who in turn resent being cut off from the economy of productive jobs. That is not a recipe for social peace.

Name Index

Subject Index